# DATE DUE

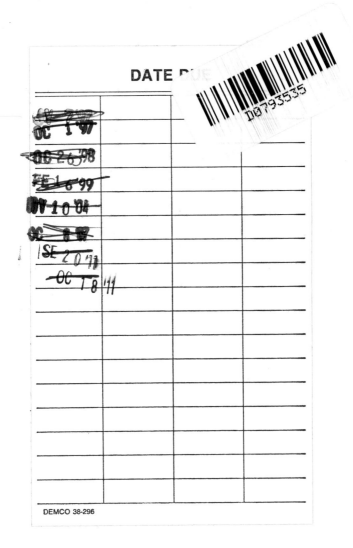

L. Sue Baugh

# Essentials of English Grammar

a practical guide
to the mastery of English

**Second Edition**

*Printed on recyclable paper*

**PASSPORT BOOKS**
a division of *NTC Publishing Group*
Lincolnwood, Illinois USA

Essentials of English Grammar
Essentials of Latin Grammar
Essentials of Russian Grammar
Essentials of Swedish Grammar
French Verbs and Essentials of Grammar
German Verbs and Essentials of Grammar
Italian Verbs and Essentials of Grammar
Spanish Verbs and Essentials of Grammar

*Also By the Same Author . . .*

Handbook for Business Writing
Handbook for Practical Letter Writing
Handbook for Memo Writing
How to Write Term Papers and Reports
Strategic Market Planning

**1995 Printing**

Published by Passport Books, a division of NTC Publishing Group,
4255 West Touhy Avenue, Lincolnwood (Chicago), Illinois 60646-1975 U.S.A.
© 1993, 1987 by NTC Publishing Group. All rights reserved.
No part of this book may be reproduced, stored in a retrieval system, or
transmitted in any form, or by any means, electronic, mechanical, photocopying
or otherwise, without the prior written permission of NTC Publishing Group.
Manufactured in the United States of America.
Library of Congress Catalog Number: 92-82677

4 5 6 7 8 9 0 VP 9 8 7 6 5 4

# Acknowledgments

I would like to thank the following people for their valuable assistance in the development of this book. Barrett Anders, Woodlands Academy of the Sacred Heart, and Dr. Robert Hausman, University of Montana, reviewed the manuscript and made many suggestions that improved the text. The copyeditor Karen Herzoff worked under exceptionally tight deadlines and did an admirable job. A special thanks to the editors at National Textbook, for their help in developing the outline and content of the book and for shepherding the project through production.

L. Sue Baugh

# Contents

## Appendixes

# Preface

*Essentials of English Grammar* is a concise guide to the basic rules of English grammar, usage, and style. It is designed to serve as a handy reference both to people who have only an occasional language question and to people who are developing the use of English as a second language. It offers quick and convenient guidance to the fundamentals of the English language.

*Essentials of English Grammar* is arranged into two main parts. *Part One, Essentials of Grammar* covers the fundamental rules and exceptions for parts of speech, punctuation, sentence construction and patterns, capitalization, abbreviations, numbers, spelling, and word division. *Part Two, Style Considerations* includes guidance on writing and combining sentences, brevity, clarity, accuracy, and gender-inclusive language. The *appendixes* offer additional resource materials.

## Part One: Essentials of Grammar

*Chapter 1.1, Parts of Speech* emphasizes the building blocks of language and their grammatical functions. Examples show proper usage of each part of speech as well as common grammatical errors to avoid. This chapter gives special attention to verb forms and tenses, a subject that is often confusing. The six basic tenses used in English are discussed, accompanied with a complete conjugation of a regular verb.

*Chapter 1.2, Punctuation and Punctuation Style* discusses how to punctuate sentences for clarity and meaning. Specific guidelines show the proper usage of each punctuation mark in a variety of situations.

*Chapter 1.3, Sentences and Sentence Patterns* describes the components that make up the English sentence and the four sentence patterns that can be used to add variety and liveliness to writing. This chapter should be particularly helpful to those who wish to develop a more expressive style.

*Chapter 1.4, Capitalization, Abbreviations, and Numbers* is a thorough coverage of these three subjects, including attention to scientific and scholarly terms not ordinarily included in a brief reference text.

*Chapter 1.5, Spelling and Word Division* addresses another topic that baffles many writers—how to spell and divide words correctly when English seems a maze of exceptions to the rules. Spelling and word division guidelines are arranged into clear, simple rules and are accompanied by ample examples. A special feature of this chapter is an abundant listing of common prefixes and suffixes used in English, including their origins, meanings, and proper spellings when joined to root words.

**Part Two: Style Considerations**

*Chapter 2.1, Sentences* contains guidelines on how to compose and combine clear, interesting and varied sentences.

*Chapter 2.2, Brevity* includes rules for the elimination of wordy and redundant language.

*Chapter 2.3, Clarity* presents guidelines to support the choice of the best words to convey meaning. It focuses on the use of specific language, parallel structures and correct references, and on eliminating or reducing jargon.

*Chapter 2.4, Accuracy* offers suggestions to help writers check facts, and other details, in their writing to ensure accurate communication.

*Chapter 2.5, Gender-Inclusive Language* offers guidelines for use of nonsexist terms, social titles, salutations, and occupational titles.

Four **Appendixes** are included for the writer's convenience:

*Appendix A* presents a list of the principal parts of the most commonly used irregular verbs.

*Appendix B* clarifies many verb-preposition combinations.

*Appendix C* provides a list of commonly confused words that sound similar but have different meanings.

*Appendix D* is a list of commonly misspelled words, presented in the correct form.

For ease of reference, *Essentials of English Grammar* includes a detailed **Table of Contents** and a carefully constructed **Index**.

# Part One:
## *Essentials of Grammar*

# 1.1 Parts of Speech

Parts of speech are the basic building blocks of language. They include nouns, pronouns, verbs, adverbs, adjectives, prepositions, interjections, and conjunctions. In this section, each part of speech is defined and its function in a sentence is discussed.

A good dictionary is an invaluable aid in understanding the pronunciation, grammatical function, spelling, and various meanings of different parts of speech. The figure below highlights the information that a dictionary offers.

An up-to-date dictionary should be part of any reference library. Consult it often for questions about spelling, grammar, or usage.

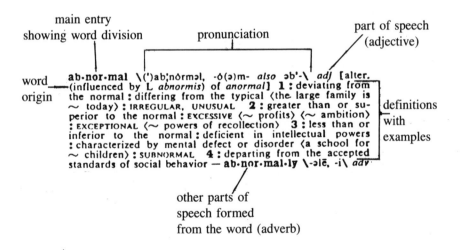

# Nouns

A *noun* refers to a person, place, or thing (objects, concepts, ideas, or events).

| *Person* | *Place* | *Thing* |
|---|---|---|
| ballplayer | stadium | glove |
| child | school | theory |
| conductor | theater | meeting |
| manager | company | excellence |

## Proper, Common, and Collective Nouns

*Proper nouns* are capitalized and name specific persons, places, or things. *Common nouns* identify general categories and are not capitalized, not even when used with proper nouns (IBM machines, Minolta cameras, Senate amendments). *Collective nouns* refer to a group of people, animals, objects, or other units.

| *Proper* | *Common* | *Collective* |
|---|---|---|
| Baker College | university | trustees |
| General Mills | company | management |
| Jane Thurgood | woman | board of directors |
| Morris | cat | litter |
| *U.S.S. Enterprise* | ship | fleet |

## Functions of Nouns

Nouns can be used as the subject, direct object, and indirect object of a verb; the object of a preposition; and an adverb or adjective. Nouns also can show possession.

| | |
|---|---|
| *Subject:* | The **mailcarrier** always rings twice. **Tulips** are early spring flowers. (Tells *who or what* does or is something.) |
| *Direct object:* | I finally sold my **car.** (Tells *what* is sold.) |
| *Indirect object:* | Harold gave the **cat** another olive. (Tells *to whom* he gave the olive.) |
| *Object of preposition:* | She gave directions **over the phone.** (Tells *what* is the object of the preposition *over.*) |
| *Adverb:* | The train leaves **today.** (Tells *when.*) |
| *Adjective:* | The **office** building faces the zoo. (Tells *what kind, which one.*) |
| *Possession:* | The **movie's** plot fooled no one. (Shows *ownership* or *possession.*) |

## Plural Nouns

Most nouns can be made plural by adding *s* to the singular form. For other plural forms such as *es* and *y* changed to *ies*, see section of Plurals on page 92.

| *Singular* | *Plural* |
|------------|----------|
| highway | highways |
| pickle | pickles |
| team | teams |

**Collective Nouns**  Collective nouns can be singular or plural depending on how they are used. When the group acts as a unit, the noun is considered singular. When the group acts as individual members, the noun is plural.

*Singular:*  The **management agrees** with the new president.

*Plural:*  The **management have expressed** different views.

*Singular:*  The **family is** celebrating three birthdays this month.

*Plural:*  The **family are** taking separate vacations.

For a fuller treatment of plural nouns, including compound and hyphenated nouns, see the section on Plurals on page 92.

## Possessive Nouns

*Possessive nouns* are used to indicate ownership or possession.

**Singular Possessive**  To form the possessive of singular nouns, add *'s* to all nouns. (For a complete discussion of the apostrophe used to indicate possession, see pages 43-44.)

| *Singular* | *Singular Possessive* |
|------------|----------------------|
| boy | the **boy's** Sony radio |
| storm | the **storm's** center |

**Plural Possessive**  To form the possessive of plural nouns that end in *s* or *es*, add an apostrophe to the end of the word.

| *Plural* | *Plural Possessive* |
|----------|---------------------|
| candles | the **candles'** light |
| ships | the **ships'** escorts |

For nouns that form the plural any other way, add *'s* to the end of the word.

| *Plural* | *Plural Possessive* |
|----------|---------------------|
| children | the **children's** toys |
| women | the **women's** department |
| men | the **men's** club |

**Singular or Plural?**    To decide whether to place the apostrophe before or after the *s,* follow this simple rule: Rephrase the sentence substituting an *of phrase* for the possessive noun to determine if the noun is singular or plural.

The (team's, teams') colors were on display.

| *Of phrase* | *Possessive form* |
|---|---|
| colors of the team (singular) | **team's** colors |
| colors of the teams (plural) | **teams'** colors |

**Individual and Joint Ownership**    To show individual ownership, make both nouns in the sentence possessive. To show joint ownership, make only the *final* noun possessive.

*Individual ownership:* **Mark's** and **Arlene's** cars were stolen. (Each person had a car that was stolen.)

*Joint ownership:* **Mark and Arlene's** car was stolen. (The car belonged to both Mark and Arlene.)

In individual ownership, the noun following the possessive is generally plural *(cars),* while in joint ownership the noun is singular *(car).* Look for this clue when deciding whether to use joint or individual possessive forms.

# Pronouns

*Pronouns* take the place of one or more nouns or a group of words in a sentence. Like nouns, they can be used to refer to a person, place, or thing.

The coach described several key plays. **He** wanted the team to memorize **them.** (*He* replaces *coach*; *them* replaces *several key plays.*).

My car, which is in the garage, is getting too old for these winters. I should sell **it.** (*It* replaces *my car, which is in the garage.*)

The word or words which the pronoun replaces are called the *antecedent* of the pronoun. In the sentences above, *coach* is the antecedent of *he,* while *my car, which is in the garage,* is the antecedent for *it.* (More about antecedents on pages 10-11.)

Pronouns are classified as *personal, intensive/reflexive, indefinite, possessive, relative, interrogative,* and *demonstrative.*

## Personal Pronouns

*Personal pronouns* can be used in a variety of ways. They serve as the subject of a sentence, the object of a verb or preposition, to show possession, for emphasis (called *intensive* pronouns), or to refer action back to the subject (called *reflexive* pronouns.).

| | |
|---|---|
| *Subject:* | **She** is simply too good to be true. |
| *Object:* | Tell **him** the parakeet died. (object of verb)<br>Break the news to **him** gently. (object of a preposition) |
| *Possessive:* | **Your** house is a landmark. Where did **his** tools go? |
| *Intensive:* | The quarterback **himself** changed the call. (The pronoun *himself* emphasizes the subject *quarterback*.) |
| *Reflexive:* | Jane taught **herself** to use the computer. We have no one to blame but **ourselves.** (The pronouns *herself* and *ourselves* refer the action back to the subjects.) |

## Case of Personal Pronouns

Personal pronouns have three cases: nominative (subject), possessive, and objective (object of verb or preposition). The following table shows the personal pronouns in all their case forms—including the intensive/reflexive forms—for the first person (*I, we*), second person (*you*), and third person (*he, she, it*).

| *Person* | *Case* | *Singular* | *Plural* |
|---|---|---|---|
| *First:* | nominative | I | we |
| | possessive | my/mine | our/ours |
| | objective | me | us |
| | intensive/<br>reflexive | myself | ourselves |
| *Second:* | nominative | you | you |
| | possessive | your/yours | your/yours |
| | objective | you | you |
| | intensive/<br>reflexive | yourself | yourselves |
| *Third:* | nominative | he/she/it | they |
| | possessive | his/her, hers/<br>its | their/theirs |
| | objective | him/her/it | them |
| | intensive/<br>reflexive | himself/<br>herself/<br>itself | themselves |

## Indefinite Pronouns

Indefinite pronouns refer to unspecified people or things. Many indefinite pronouns express some idea of quantity: *all, several, few, none*. Following is a list of the most commonly used indefinite pronouns.

| | | | |
|---|---|---|---|
| all | each | most | other |
| another | either | neither | several |
| any | everybody | nobody | some |
| anybody | everyone | none | somebody |
| anyone | few | no one | someone |
| both | many | one | such |

The board of directors needed a new president for the company. They appointed **someone** from outside the firm. (*Someone* replaces *new president.*)

Do you have any Western novels in your library? Yes, we have a **few.** (*Few* replaces *Western novels.*)

## Possessive Pronouns

*Possessive pronouns,* unlike possessive nouns, never take an apostrophe. As shown in the table (on page 7), the possessive forms are *my/mine, our/ours, your/yours, his/her, hers/its, their/theirs.* The pronoun *who* also has a possessive form, *whose.*

**Whose** gym shoes are on the floor?

I thought **my** wallet was lost, but the one Jameel found was **mine.**

**Our** vacation starts next week. Those sad-looking plants are **ours.**

How can we get **your** dog to obey? Is this **yours?**

George Burns never seems to lose **his** timing.

You have to take either **her** book or **theirs. Hers** is better.

The lawyers knew **their** client was probably guilty.

**Possessive Pronouns vs. Contractions**    People often confuse possessive pronouns with pronoun-verb forms that sound exactly like them *(its/it's, whose/who's, your/you're, their/they're).* To keep the possessive forms straight, remember this easy rule: Possessive pronouns never take an apostrophe.

Pronouns that do take an apostrophe are contractions formed by the pronoun and a verb *(it's = it is; they're = they are).*

| | |
|---|---|
| *its:* | The rocket fired **its** engines. (possessive) |
| *it's:* | **It's** *(it is)* an awesome sight. (contraction) |
| *whose:* | **Whose** tape recorder is this? (possessive) |
| *who's:* | We need to know **who's** *(who is)* coming. (contraction) |
| | **Who's** *(who has)* been eating my fudge? (contraction) |
| *your:* | Can he use **your** telescope? (possessive) |
| *you're:* | **You're** *(you are)* six years too late. (contraction) |
| *their:* | The Alfa Romeo is **their** best car. (possessive) |
| *they're:* | **They're** *(they are)* the top racing team. (contraction) |

**Possessive Pronouns and Gerunds**    *Gerunds* are verb forms ending in *-ing* that are used as nouns. In the sentence *Skiing is a wonderful sport, skiing* is a gerund used as the subject. If a pronoun precedes the gerund, the pronoun is generally in the possessive form.

Bill told me about **his driving** 900 miles in one day.

She liked **my calling** her before I came over.

**Carol's winning** the sweepstakes stunned us all.

The exception to this rule occurs when the pronoun follows verbs like *see, hear,* and *watch.* In that case, use the objective form of the pronoun.

> We didn't see **him leaving** the house.
> The whole neighborhood heard **us playing** R.E.M.

## Relative Pronouns

*Relative pronouns* can be used to avoid repeating the noun within a sentence. They are particularly helpful when one clause is embedded in another, because they keep both clauses grammatical.

The relative pronouns *who, whom,* and *whose* refer to people and animals, while *which* and *of which* refer to things. *That* can refer to people or things.

> The violin, **which** he learned to play as a child, is a valuable instrument. (Avoids repeating the noun—*The violin—the violin he learned to play.*)
> The woman **who** bought the suit returned it the next day. (*The woman she* would be ungrammatical.)

## Interrogative Pronouns

The interrogative pronouns *who, whom, whose, what,* and *which* introduce questions. *Who, whom,* and *whose* indicate that the question refers to a person or animal; *what* refers to an object, idea, or event; and *which* can indicate either a person or thing.

> **Who** called last night?
> **What** is your earliest memory?
> I have a pen and pencil. **Which** do you want?

## Demonstrative Pronouns

*Demonstrative pronouns* generally indicate nearness to or distance from the speaker, either literally or symbolically. *This, these, that,* and *those* usually refer to a specific noun, pronoun, or clause. However, sometimes the reference is to a general class of people or objects rather than to a specific antecedent.

> **This** is my driver's license, and **that** is my credit card. (The driver's license is closer at hand.)
> I don't envy **those** caught out in the storm tonight. (*Those* has no specific antecedent but refers to a general class of people: anyone caught out in the storm.)

## Pronoun-Antecedent Agreement

The *antecedent,* as mentioned previously, is the word or phrase to which a pronoun refers. Pronouns must agree with their antecedents in person, case, and number.

*Agreement in Person*

*Incorrect:* The programmer should know BASIC thoroughly. Otherwise, **you** will have trouble writing programs. (The pronoun *you* is in the second person, while its antecedent *programmer* is in the third person. Therefore the correct pronoun is the third person *he* or *she*.)

*Correct:* The programmer should know BASIC thoroughly. Otherwise, **he or she** will have trouble writing programs.

*Agreement in Case*

*Incorrect:* Is that Cherryl and Donna by the car?
Yes, it's **them.** (The objective case *them* is incorrect. The nominative case *they* is the correct form, even though it may sound strange to your ears.)

*Correct:* Is that Cherryl and Donna by the car?
Yes, it's **they.**

*Agreement in Number*

*Incorrect:* The data are obsolete and should be replaced. We can't use **it** any longer. (The plural noun *data* is the antecedent and requires the plural pronoun *them*.)

*Correct:* The data are obsolete and should be replaced. We can't use **them** any longer.

**Imprecise Use of Pronouns**   Pronouns should refer to a specific antecedent. Many writers misuse the pronouns *this, that, which, it,* and *they* by making them refer to entire sentences or ideas. Such errors can confuse the reader and must be avoided.

*Vague:* He wanted to raise the walls, put on the roof, and hang the doors all in one day. **This** was unrealistic. (The pronoun *this* refers to the sentence and not to any specific antecedent.)

*Precise:* His schedule was to raise the walls, put on the roof, and hang the doors all in one day. **This** was unrealistic. (The pronoun now refers to the antecedent *schedule*.)

*Vague:* The engineer asked for a meeting to discuss the new contract. I told her we couldn't do **that.** (The antecedent for the pronoun *that* is unclear. Is it the meeting or the discussion that the speaker is declining?)

*Precise:* The engineer asked if we could meet at her office. I told her we couldn't do **that.** (In this sentence *that* refers to the clause *if we could meet at her office*.)

**Double Antecedents**   When *and* joins two antecedents, use a plural pronoun. If the antecedents are joined by *nor* or *or,* or when they form a unit (*ham and eggs*), use a singular pronoun.

**An elm and a maple tree** cast **their** shadows across the lawn.

Neither **Harriet nor Claire** has **her** car today.

**Research and Development** had **its** budget slashed this year.

## Who or Whom?

The confusion over when to use *who* or *whom* has bothered writers for many years. In modern usage, the trend has been to drop the more formal-sounding *whom* and to use *who* in all cases. Following are the rules for using these two pronouns.

**1. *Who* is used as the subject of a sentence or a clause (group of words containing a subject and verb) and never as an object.**

**Who** said we wouldn't have a rest period?   (*Who* is the subject of the sentence.)

Can you tell **who** is playing the drums?   (*Who* is the subject of the clause.)

That job goes to **whoever** walks through the door first.   (*Whoever* is the subject of the clause.)

**2. *Whom* is always used in the objective case as the object of a verb or preposition. It is never used as the subject.**

Address the letter "To **Whom** It May Concern."   (*Whom* is the object of the preposition *to.*)

**Whom** did you ask to pick up the order?   (*Whom* is the object of the verb *ask.*)

Are there any dealers **whom** you would recommend?   (*You* is the subject of the verb *recommend; whom* is the object of that verb.)

The job goes to **whomever** you call first. (*Whomever* is the object of the verb *call. You* is the subject. Compare this sentence with the one using *whoever.*)

# Verbs

*Verbs* are words or groups of words that express action or a state of being or condition. They provide the power or drive for sentences.

They **smashed** through the door.   (action)

The ambassador **filed** a formal protest.   (action)

The child **seems** unhappy today.   (state of being)

The car **handles** well.   (condition)

Verbs that express a state of being or condition are called *linking verbs*. These verbs link the subject with a noun, pronoun, or adjective that describes or identifies it. The word or words linked to the subject are referred to as a *subject complement*. In general, a verb is a linking verb if it can be substituted for some form of the verb *seem*.

You **look** *(seem)* calm enough—are you?
She **felt** *(seemed)* ill at ease in the doctor's office.

The most common linking verb is *be* and its forms *am, is, are, was, were, being,* and *been.* Other common linking verbs include the following:

*Common Linking Verbs*

| | | | |
|---|---|---|---|
| appear | grow | remain | sound |
| become | hear | seem | stay |
| feel | look | smell | taste |

## Basic Verb Forms

A few verb forms are the basis for all verb tenses and phrases. These forms are as follows:

| | |
|---|---|
| *Base form:* | Children **play** in the park. |
| *Infinitive:* | Tell them **to play** here. |
| *Past tense:* | They **played** all day yesterday. |
| *Past participle:* | He has **played** too long. |
| *Present participle:* | I am **playing** with her today. |
| *Gerund (noun form):* | **Playing** is children's "work." |

## Auxiliary Verbs

The past and present participles of the verb are also part of a word group that comprises a complete verb form: *has played, am playing.* The verbs used with these participles are called *auxiliary verbs* (also known as *helping verbs*). They signal a change in tense (*he walked; he has walked*) or a change in voice (*we told; we were told*). Following is a list of the most commonly used auxiliary verbs.

| *Auxiliary* | *Auxiliary + Main Verb* |
|---|---|
| has/have | The jury **has rendered** a verdict. |
| | The defendants **have heard** the sentence. |
| is/are | The satellite **is boosting** the signal. |
| | They **are receiving** it in Hawaii. |
| can/could | He **can operate** in the morning. |
| | The patient **could come** home in a week. |
| should/would | The flight **should land** in New Jersey. |
| | We **would like** to arrive in New York. |

| do/did | I **do want** to win.<br>I **did practice** all week. |
|---|---|
| will/shall | I **will tell** them to take the furniture away.<br>**Shall** we **buy** the stuffed moose? |
| must/ought | They **must report** the faulty switch.<br>She **ought to call** the head office. |

## Verb Tenses

Verb tenses allow us to talk about time, to place an action or state of being in the past, present, or future (*I called, I call/I am calling, I will call*). They also permit communication of intention, what would, could, or should be done (*I would have called, I can call, I will have called*).

Learning to use the right verb tense is important to convey intentions and the time of an action or state of being accurately and clearly. The various tenses in English are formed using the basic elements of the verb.

| | |
|---|---|
| *Base form:* | march |
| *Past tense:* | marched |
| *Present participle:* | marching |
| *Past participle:* | marched |
| *Auxiliary verbs:* | am (was) marching, have (had) marched, will march |

English has regular and irregular verbs. Learn the basic verb forms of these words to create the proper tenses and to avoid mixing tenses in writing.

## Regular Verbs

*Regular verbs* follow the same pattern when moving from one tense to another. English has six basic tenses: *present, past, future, present perfect, past perfect,* and *future perfect*. In addition, the progressive and conditional forms are used for special functions. The *progressive form* (*I am singing, I was singing, I will be singing*) is used to indicate continuity of action, while the *conditional form* (*I can sing, I could sing, I could have sung*) conveys intention to do or be something.

Following is a complete conjugation of the verb *to watch*. The function of each tense is discussed following the conjugation.

*Present Tense*

| I watch | we watch |
|---|---|
| you watch | you watch |
| he/she/it watches | they watch |

| | |
|---|---|
| *Present progressive:* | I am (you are) watching, etc. |
| *Present conditional:* | I can (I could) watch, etc. |

*Past Tense*
(base form of the verb + -*d* or -*ed*)

| | |
|---|---|
| I watched | we watched |
| you watched | you watched |
| he/she/it watched | they watched |

*Past progressive:*     I was watching, etc.
*Past conditional:*     I could have watched, etc.
                        I could have been watching, etc.

*Future Tense*
(*will* or *shall* + the base form of the verb)

| | |
|---|---|
| I will (shall) watch | we will (shall) watch |
| you will watch | you will watch |
| he/she/it will watch | they will watch |

*Future progressive:*     I will (shall) be watching, etc.

*Present Perfect Tense*
(*have* or *has* + the past participle)

| | |
|---|---|
| I have watched | we have watched |
| you have watched | you have watched |
| he/she/it has watched | they have watched |

*Progressive form:*     I have been watching, etc.

*Past Perfect Tense*
(*had* + the past participle)

| | |
|---|---|
| I had watched | we had watched |
| you had watched | you had watched |
| he/she/it had watched | they had watched |

*Progressive form:*     I had been watching, etc.

*Future Perfect Tense*
(*will have* or *shall have* + the past participle)

| | |
|---|---|
| I will (shall) have watched | we will (shall) have watched |
| you will have watched | you will have watched |
| he/she/it will have watched | they will have watched |

*Progressive form:*     I will have been watching, etc.

## Uses of the Six Tenses

**Present Tense**   The present tense is used to express an action or to state a fact that is occurring at the present time. The present tense also can be formed using auxiliary verbs for emphasis or to express intention.

I **live** here.

I **am living** here.   (progressive form)

I **do live** here.   (emphatic form)

I **can live** here.   (conditional)

The present tense also is used to indicate habitual action or something that is true at all times.

She **goes** out every evening.
My grandfather believed that silence **is** (instead of *was*) golden.

Writers occasionally use the present tense when reviewing the contents of a book or describing past events to bring them vividly to life for the reader. This form of the present tense is known as the *literary or historical present*.

In his book on Alexander the Great, the Greek historian Arrian **dismisses** romantic legend and **concentrates** on sifting truth from fiction.

**Progressive Form**   The progressive form emphasizes the continuity of an action rather than its completion. For example, compare *I wrote a letter* with *I was writing a letter*. The first sentence simply states an action that was completed in the past, while the second sentence implies that the action is connected to another event. Adverbs are often used with progressive tenses to stress the continuous nature of the action or state of being (*He is* **always** *singing in the shower*). Progressive forms can be used with all six tenses.

**Past Tense**   The past tense is used to express action or to help make a statement about something that occurred in the past and has not continued into the present.

I **lived** there.
I **was living** there while I was in school.   (progressive)
I **did live** there.   (emphatic)

**Future Tense**   The future tense is used to express an action or to help make a statement about something that will occur in the future.

I **will (shall)** live there.
I **will be living** there.   (progressive)
I **am going to be living** there.   (progressive)
I **can be living** there.   (conditional)

The distinction between *will* and *shall* is no longer observed by most people. The two verbs can be used interchangeably for the simple future in the first person. However, in a few expressions, *shall* is the only form used.

**Shall** we go to the movie?
**Shall** I put the box here?

To use *will* in these sentences would change the meaning. However, except for these special uses, *will* and *shall* are equally correct.

**Perfect Tenses**    Perfect tenses describe actions or states of being that happened at one time but are seen in relation to another time. For example, *I gave a donation to the Girl Scouts* is a simple statement about a past event and would be used to tell someone what happened in the past. *I have given a donation to the Girl Scouts* connects the past event to the present and can be used to imply a habitual or continuous action.

*Present Perfect Tense.*    The present perfect tense is used to express an action or to help make a statement about something occurring at an indefinite time in the past or something that has occurred in the past and continues into the present.

> I **have lived** here for a long time.
> I **have lived** here for three months.   (The speaker is still living there.)
> I **have been living** here for three months.   (progressive)
> I **could have been living** here instead of where I am now.   (conditional)

*Past Perfect Tense.*    The past perfect tense is used to express an action or to help make a statement about something completed in the past before some other past action or event.

> After I **had lived** here for three months, they raised the rent.
> After I **had been living** here for three months, they raised the rent.   (progressive)

*Future Perfect Tense.*    The future perfect tense is used to express an action or to help make a statement about something that will be completed in the future before some other future action or event.

> By this October, I **will have lived here** for six months.
> By this October, I **will have been living** here for six months.   (progressive)

## Irregular Verbs

*Irregular verbs* follow no fixed rules for forming the various past, present, and future tenses. You simply have to memorize them or consult your dictionary. Some of the most commonly used irregular verbs are listed in Appendix A on page 125. Below are a few examples of common irregular verbs which show the variety of their forms.

| Base Form | Past Tense | Past Participle | Present Participle |
|---|---|---|---|
| be | was | been | being |
| break | broke | broken | breaking |
| fly | flew | flown | flying |
| lie | lay | lain | lying |
| ring | rang | rung | ringing |

# Common Errors in Using Verb Tenses

People often mix their tenses or use the wrong verb form when speaking. Although these errors may be overlooked in conversation, they are painfully evident in written communication. They often confuse the reader and affect the tone of the message. Study the following incorrect and correct sentences:

### 1. Use the correct verb form with each tense.

*Incorrect:*    He checked on the shipment and **has went** to pick it up.

*Correct:*    He checked on the shipment and **has gone** to pick it up. (*Gone* is the past participle of the verb *to go* and is the correct form to use with the auxiliary verb *has. Went* is the past tense form and is incorrect.)

*Incorrect:*    I **done** the work last night and handed it in this morning.

*Correct:*    I **did** the work last night and handed it in this morning. (*Done,* the past participle, is incorrect—the verb should be in the simple past tense *did.*)

*Incorrect:*    Barb and Louise **have ordered** the tickets, **wrote** their friends about the concert, and **gave** away pictures of the band.

*Correct:*    Barb and Louise **have ordered** the tickets, **written** their friends about the concert, and **given** away pictures of the band. (The auxiliary verb *have* requires the past participle for each verb in this sentence—*have ordered, [have] written, [have] given. Wrote* and *gave* are the past tense forms of the verbs and are incorrect.)

*Incorrect:*    The book **is** fascinating reading. It **provided** a detailed study of how cultures **were created.**

*Correct:*    The book **is** fascinating reading. It **provides** a detailed study of how cultures **are created.** (The writer refers to the book in the present tense in the first sentence. All references that follow should also be in the literary or historical present tense.)

### 2. Use the past perfect tense for the earlier of two past actions.

When describing two events in the past that did not occur at the same time, use the past perfect tense to refer to the event or action in the more distant past.

*Incorrect:*    I suddenly **remembered** (past) that I **left** (more distant past) my purse at the office. (Since leaving the purse at the office preceded remembering the fact, the past perfect form of *left* should be used.)

*Correct:*    I suddenly **remembered** (past) that I **had left** (past perfect) my purse at the office.

*Incorrect:*    An airport **now existed** (past) where a city dump **was** (more distant past). (Using the past tense for both verbs suggests that the airport and city dump are there together.)

*Correct:*    An airport **now existed** (past) where a city dump **had been** (past perfect). (The past perfect makes it clear that the city dump preceded the airport.)

**3. Do not use *would have* in "if clauses" that express the earlier of two past actions. Use the past perfect.**

*Incorrect:*    If he **would have thought** of it, he would have asked you to ride with us.

*Correct:*    If he **had thought** of it, he would have asked you to ride with us.

*Incorrect*    If I **would have studied** harder, I'd have made the academic quiz team.

*Correct:*    If I **had studied** harder, I'd have made the academic quiz team.

**4. Use the present infinitive (*to play, to see*, etc.) to express action *following* another action.**

*Incorrect:*    I was disappointed because I had hoped **to have gone** with you. (Did the speaker hope *to have gone* or *to go*? The present infinitive *to go* is the correct form because the action it expresses follows the verb *had hoped*.)

*Correct:*    I was disappointed because I had hoped **to go** with you.

*Incorrect:*    She intended **to have visited** all her relatives. (Did she intend *to have visited* or *to visit?*)

*Correct:*    She intended **to visit** all her relatives.

**5. Use the perfect infinitive (*to have written, to have seen*, etc.) to express action *before* another action.**

*Correct:*    He was happy **to have seen** Ralph. (The speaker saw Ralph first, then he was happy about seeing him. Therefore, the perfect infinitive *to have seen* is the proper form to use.)

**6. In participial phrases, use *having* with the past participle to express action before another action.**

*Incorrect:*    **Giving** my bike to George, I couldn't ride to the beach that afternoon. (The present participle *giving* is incorrectly used to express an action completed before the second action in the sentence.)

*Correct:*    **Having given** my bike to George, I couldn't ride to the beach that afternoon.

| | |
|---|---|
| *Incorrect:* | **Painting** the front porch, he slept the rest of the day. (He had to paint the porch before he could go to sleep.) |
| *Correct:* | **Having painted** the front porch, he slept the rest of the day. (This could also be expressed by saying *After painting the front porch, he slept all day.*) |

## Mood

Verbs can be used to express differences in the intention or *mood* of the speaker or writer. There are three moods in English: the indicative, imperative, and subjunctive moods. Each one has a specific function.

The *indicative mood* is used when the speaker or writer wishes to make a statement or ask a question.

**Are** you **leaving** tonight?

The train **is running** ten minutes late.

The *imperative mood* is used for commands, requests, or directions.

**Call** Fredericks and **cancel** that shipment.

Please **return** the book when you are finished.

**Turn** right at the corner, then **go** left.

The *subjunctive mood* uses a different form of the past and present to express matters of urgency, formality, possibility, or speculation.

| | |
|---|---|
| *Urgency:* | I demanded that she **see** me immediately. (The indicative mood would use the form *sees* or *can see*—for example, I want to know if she *can see* me immediately.) |
| *Formality:* | He recommended that the zoning law **be** adopted. (The subjunctive mood uses *be adopted* rather than the indicative mood *is adopted*—for example, the vote is 44 to 3; the law *is adopted.*) |
| *Possibility:* | If I **were** to sign the invoice, we could not refuse any defective parts. (The phrase *If I were to sign* expresses a future possibility. It has no reference to the past, even though *were* is a past tense verb form. Compare this sentence to *Because I signed the invoice, we could not refuse any defective parts.* In this sentence, the indicative mood describes an action that took place in the past.) |
| *Speculation:* | If he **were** king, he would decree that football be played every afternoon. (The subjunctive mood expresses something that is not true, a statement contrary to fact. The indicative mood, on the other hand, simply states a fact—for example, *If he was ready, why didn't he come?*) |

## Active and Passive Voice

If the subject of a sentence performs an action, the verb is in the *active voice*. If the subject receives the action, the verb is in the *passive voice*.

> *Active voice:*    She **gave** a contribution (The subject *she* performs the action.)
>
> *Passive voice:*    She **was given** a contribution. (The subject *she* receives the action.)
>
> *Active voice:*    We **have delivered** the mail.
>
> *Passive voice:*    The mail **was delivered** to us. (*Mail* is now the subject and receives the action.)

The active voice adds interest and liveliness to a message. In general, use the active voice. Avoid weak and awkward passive verb constructions or long passages in which all the verbs are passive.

The passive voice, however, does have its contribution to make. It can be used to express an action in which the actor is unknown, when a more objective or diplomatic tone is required, or when it is desirable not to disclose the actor.

> *Active voice:*    Jim **locked** the door before we arrived home.
>
> *Passive voice:*    The door **had been locked** before we arrived home.
>
> *Active voice:*    We **have examined** your application and **must decline** your request for credit.
>
> *Passive voice:*    Your application **has been reviewed** and at this time your request for credit **must be declined.**
>
> *Active voice:*    Our sales manager **has made** a mistake in completing your order.
>
> *Passive voice:*    A mistake **has been made** in completing your order.

In the second example, the passive voice emphasizes the recipient of the action and minimizes the writer's role. Using the passive voice can make the decision seem less personally directed toward the reader. The speaker can then discuss the reasons for declining the application.

## Subject-Verb Agreement

Just as pronouns must agree with their antecedents in person, case, and number, verbs also must agree with their subjects in person and in number.

The *first person subject* is the person or persons speaking in a sentence (*I, we*). The *second person subject* is the person or persons addressed (*you, you*). The *third person subject* refers to the person or thing spoken about and may be any noun or third-person pronoun (*he, she, they*).

*Agreement in Person*

*First:*  **I am** hot. **We are** cold.

*Second:*  **You return** the book.

*Third:*  The **car rusts. She drives** fast. **They laugh** a lot.

Verbs agree with their subjects in number. Therefore, a singular subject takes a singular verb; a plural subject takes a plural verb.

*Agreement in Number*

| *Singular* | *Plural* |
|---|---|
| The **window is** open. | The **windows are** open. |
| **She writes** quickly. | **They write** quickly. |
| **I am** going home. | **We are** going home. |
| **You gave** a lesson. | **All of you gave** a lesson. |

## Special Subject-Verb Agreement Cases

Compound subjects, collective nouns, and plural nouns used as titles of courses or subject areas can create confusion regarding subject-verb agreement. Following are guidelines for using a singular or plural verb in such cases.

**Compound Subjects Joined by *and*—Singular Verb**   Use the singular verbs for compound subjects joined by *and* 1) when the subject is considered a unit (research and development) and 2) when both parts of the subject are modified by *each* or *every.*

The **secretary and treasurer has** filed the minutes.

**Each** owner and **every** pet **receives** a prize for entering our pet show.

**Compound Subjects Joined by *and*—Plural Verb**   Except for the cases already noted, compound subjects joined by *and* take a plural verb.

**Rain and hail were falling** at the same time.

**Tom and Samira have resigned** over this matter.

There **are one book and two paintings** on the floor.

**Are the computer and the typewriter** both IBM?

**Compound Subjects Joined by *or* or *nor*—Singular Verb**   Use the singular verb 1) if the subject next to the verb is considered singular or 2) if both parts of the subject are singular.

The **drawers or the closet is** the place to look.

**Is** the **horse or the pony** loose again?

**Neither** Alan **nor** Julie **remembers** borrowing my car.

**Compound Subjects Joined by *or* or *nor*—Plural Verb**    The plural verb is used if the subject nearest the verb is plural or if both parts of the subject are plural.

> The **closet or the drawers are** the place to look.
>
> The **directors or the producers receive** all the credit.
>
> **Neither** the girls **nor** their teachers **were** aware of the approaching high tide.

**Plural Nouns—Singular Verbs**    Plural nouns used as the titles of courses or subject areas or as measurements or units of quantity (dollars, pounds, inches) take a singular verb.

> **Humanities has** a long, involved reading list.
>
> I weighed myself, and **twelve pounds has** to go!
>
> **Forty miles seems** a long way to walk in one day.
>
> **Is $2,500** a good price for this car?

**Collective Nouns—Singular or Plural Verbs**    To emphasize the collective noun as a unit, use the singular verb. To refer to individuals within the group, use the plural verb.

> The **fleet sails** tomorrow at 04:30.
>
> The **Seventh Fleet have** three days to repair their vessels.
>
> Everyone applauds how hard the **council works.**
>
> **The council are** divided about the tax reform issue.
>
> When **is the team** going to play its next home game?
>
> **The team need** to recuperate from their injuries.

**Prepositional Phrases and Other Matters Set Off from the Subject**    Prepositional phrases following the subject or material set off from the subject by commas generally does not influence subject-verb agreement. To decide whether to use a singular or plural verb form, simply block out the prepositional phrase or additional material and look only at the subject and verb.

> **None** of the facts **has been proven** true. (*None* ~~of the facts~~ *has*)
>
> **Any** of these students **writes** well. (*Any* [one] ~~of these students~~ *writes*)
>
> Many **flowers,** such as the tulip, **grow** in northern climates. (Many *flowers,* ~~such as the tulip,~~ *grow*)
>
> My **house,** unlike those houses, **looks** brand new. (My *house,* ~~unlike those houses,~~ *looks*)

The exception to this rule occurs when the word *all* is followed by a singular or plural noun or pronoun. In this case, the prepositional phrase or material following *all* will determine whether to use a singular or plural verb.

> **All** of my apple pie **was eaten.**    (Singular *pie* takes the singular verb *was eaten.*)
>
> **All** of my apple pies **were eaten.**    (Plural *pies* take the plural verb *were eaten.*)

# Adjectives

*Adjectives* modify nouns, pronouns, and other adjectives. They provide pertinent information about the words they modify by answering the questions *What kind? How many? Which one? How much?* When used well, adjectives can add precision, color, and a dash of originality to writing.

> We need a **two-year-old male** leopard.   (What kind?)
>
> There are **nine** planets in our solar system.   (How many?)
>
> He gave her **that** box over there.   (Which one?)
>
> I have a **larger** paycheck than he does.   (How much?)

## Demonstrative Adjectives

The demonstrative adjectives *which, what, this, these, that,* and *those* are used to emphasize which items are being singled out and their distance from the speaker. Unlike the pronoun forms of these words, demonstrative adjectives are never used alone.

> I feel sorry for **those** people caught in the flood.   (Pronoun form: I feel sorry for *those* caught in the flood.)
>
> Take **this** car here and **that** car over by the driveway and park them both in the lot.
>
> I don't understand **which** person you're talking about.
>
> **What** schedule is the driver using this week?

## Limiting Adjectives

Many adjectives are used to identify or number the nouns they modify. In nearly all cases, the limiting adjective comes before the noun. Following is a list of some of the more common of these adjectives.

| Limiting Adjective | Noun |
|---|---|
| a/an | **a** pineapple, **an** orange |
| the | **the** wrench, **the** screwdrivers |
| few | **few** shells |
| many | **many** bubbles |
| every | **every** hour |
| each | **each** dime |
| both | **both** presents |
| several | **several** monkeys |
| some | **some** pasta |
| any | **any** person |
| most | **most** ideas |
| one | **one** song |

Limiting adjectives *a, an,* and *the* are also known as *articles. A* and *an* are *indefinite articles* and refer to an unspecified item in a class (*a box, an apple*). *The* is a *definite article* and refers to one or more specific items in a class (*the box, the apples*).

## Comparisons

Adjectives also are used to show comparisons between or among persons, places, or things. The positive, comparative, and superlative forms represent different degrees of a quality or characteristic.

The *positive* form is the base word (*low, cautious*). The *comparative* is formed by adding the suffix *-er* or the word *more* (*lower, more cautious*). The *superlative* requires the suffix *-est* or the word *most* (*lowest, most cautious*).

| *Positive* | *Comparative* | *Superlative* |
|---|---|---|
| careful | more careful | most careful |
| jealous | more jealous | most jealous |
| proud | prouder | proudest |
| soft | softer | softest |

There are several irregular comparative forms as well.

| | | |
|---|---|---|
| bad | worse | worst |
| far | farther | farthest |
| good | better | best |

When comparing two items, use the positive and comparative forms. For more than two items, use the superlative.

The black puppy is **smaller** than its brother.　(comparative)

The brown puppy is the **smallest** of the eight.　(superlative)

Jan has a **good** grade point average, Brian has a **better** one, while Joan has the **best** average of all.　(positive, comparative, superlative)

That movie was **more** boring than a test pattern.　(comparative)

He has the **most** expensive car on the block.　(superlative)

## Compound Adjectives

*Compound adjectives* generally are hyphenated when they precede the noun they modify. When they follow the noun, they are two words.

She designed a **blue-gray** living room set.

She designed a living room set that was **blue gray.**

That is a **past-due** bill.

The bill is **past due.**

## Predicate Adjectives

When an adjective follows a linking verb such as *feel, become, seem, get, is, look,* and *smell,* the word complements the verb and is known as a *predicate adjective.* The adjective does not modify the verb but refers to the condition of the subject.

> She looks **beautiful.**
> He seems **ill.** Is he **all right?**
> The water is getting **hot.**

# Adverbs

*Adverbs* modify verbs, adjectives, and other adverbs. They answer the questions *When? Where? How much?* or *How?* Adverbs describe an action or state of being in greater detail and can provide a more vivid picture of what is happening.

> She **always** signs her name with "Ms."   (When?)
> They put the children **downstairs.**   (Where?)
> Knead the dough **slowly.**   (How?)
> I objected **mildly** to the suggestion.   (How much?)

## Forming Adverbs

Most adverbs end in *-ly* and can be formed from the adjective. In some cases, however, the adjective and adverb both end in *-ly.*

| Noun | Adjective | Adverb |
|------|-----------|--------|
| care | careful | carefully |
| collect | collective | collectively |
| coward | cowardly | cowardly |
| hour | hourly | hourly |
| thought | thoughtful | thoughtfully |

## Types of Adverbs

Many adverbs do not end in *-ly.* Those indicating direction, place, time, or degree look the same as nouns, prepositions, or adjectives. Following are examples of these different types of adverbs, including those ending in *-ly.*

*Adverbs of Time/Frequency (When?)*

| | | |
|------|------|------|
| always | frequently | occasionally |
| before | never | often |
| eventually | now | once |
| forever | Monday | seldom |

### *Adverbs of Place/Direction (Where?)*

| | | |
|---|---|---|
| across | in | there |
| around | out | through |
| backwards | over | under |
| here | sideways | upstairs |

### *Adverbs of Degree (How much?)*

| | | |
|---|---|---|
| completely | less | nearly |
| entirely | mildly | somewhat |
| excessively | most | thoroughly |
| however | much | |

### *Adverbs of Manner (How?)*

| | | |
|---|---|---|
| beautifully | equally | orderly |
| carefully | handily | quickly |
| coldly | hotly | resentfully |
| earnestly | nicely | tirelessly |

## Comparisons

Adverbs—like adjectives—are used in comparisons. The *positive* is the base word (*fast, softly*). The *comparative* is formed by adding *-er* or the word *more* (*faster, more softly*), and the superlative by adding *-est* or the word *most* (*fastest, most softly*). A few adverbs have irregular forms (*well, better, best*).

He drives himself **hard.**   (positive)

He drives himself **harder** than I think he should.   (comparative)

He drives himself the **hardest** of anyone I know.   (superlative)

I write **well** with others in the room.   (positive)

I write **better** when I'm alone.   (comparative)

I write **best** late at night.   (superlative)

The tiger moves **quietly** through the jungle.   (positive)

The tiger moves **more quietly** than the deer.   (comparative)

The tiger moves the **most quietly** of the three big cats.   (superlative)

## Adverb Position and Meaning

The position of the adverb can affect the meaning of the sentence. The most common error involves misplacing the adverb *only.* Make sure that the adverb position conveys what you intend to say.

*Unclear:*   We **only** walked to the store and not to the bank. (Did the speakers only walk and not run? Or did they walk only to the store and not elsewhere? The meaning is unclear.)

*Clear:*   We walked **only** to the store and not to the bank.

> *Unclear:*   She **frequently** calls the magazine editor.   (Does she call the magazine editor more frequently than anyone else? Or does she simply call the editor many times [frequently]?)
>
> *Clear:*   She calls the magazine editor **frequently.**

In general, avoid splitting the verb phrase when using an adverb. While this rule is not carved in stone, it is a good one to keep in mind.

> *Avoid:*   I have **also** given the matter my attention.
> *Better:*   I **also** have given the matter my attention.
>
> *Avoid:*   He had **accurately** filled out the form.
> *Better:*   He had filled out the form **accurately.**

## Adjective or Adverb?

Some words function as either adverbs or adjectives, and many writers may confuse them. Among the most troublesome words are *good, well, badly,* and *bad.*

*Good* is an adjective and is always used as an adjective, never an adverb.

> You've done a **good** job on that garden.   (modifies *job*)
> I feel **good.**   (complements verb *feel* and refers to the condition of the subject)

*Well* is both an adjective, meaning in good health, and an adverb of manner, answering the question *how* something is done. Never use *good* to modify a verb.

> I feel **well.**   (complements verb *feel* and refers to the condition of subject)
> The reporter handled that story **well.**   (modifies verb *handled*)
> She types **well.**   (modifies verb *types*)
> (She types **good** is incorrect.)

The adverb *badly* is often mistaken for the adjective *bad.* Badly, an adverb of manner, indicates that something is done ineptly or poorly. It often follows an action verb.

> He plays the piano **badly.**   (modifies the verb *plays* and answers the question: *How does he play the piano? Badly.*)
> They painted the fence **badly.**   (modifies the verb *painted* and answers the question: *How did they paint the fence? Badly.*)

The adjective *bad* means "in poor spirits" or is used to describe the degree of something. When it follows a linking verb, it is a predicate adjective describing the condition of the subject.

> I feel **bad.**   (predicate adjective referring to the condition of the subject *I*)
> That was a **bad** mistake.   (adjective modifying *mistake*)

Never write *I feel badly* or *You look badly* when referring to the condition of the subject. These statements say that you feel (touch someone or something) poorly or that someone looks (sees things) poorly.

# Prepositions

*Prepositions* are connecting words that show the relationship among words in a sentence. Nouns, pronouns, gerund phrases, or noun clauses can be the objects of prepositions. Together with the preposition they form a *prepositional phrase.* These phrases serve as adjectives modifying nouns and pronouns or as adverbs modifying verbs, adjectives, or other adverbs.

> Put it **in** the box.   (The noun *box* is the object of *in;* the prepositional phrase serves as an adverb and modifies the verb *put.*)
>
> Give this to the usher **on** the right.   (The noun *right* is the object of *on;* the phrase is used as an adjective, modifying the noun *usher.*)
>
> **After** telling them a story, he put the children to bed.   (The gerund phrase *telling them a story* is the object of the preposition *after.*)
>
> **Because of** what they told us, we cut our trip short.   (The noun clause *what they told us* is the object of the preposition *because of.*)

Following is a list of some of the most commonly used prepositions.

| | | |
|---|---|---|
| about | between | off |
| above | beyond | on |
| across | by | over |
| after | down | since |
| against | during | through |
| along | except | to |
| among | for | toward |
| around | from | under |
| at | in | until |
| before | inside | up |
| behind | into | upon |
| below | like | with |
| beneath | near | within |
| beside | of | without |

## Phrasal Prepositions

Although most prepositions are one word, some consist of phrases and are called *phrasal prepositions*. They are used frequently in spoken and written communication.

| | | |
|---|---|---|
| because of | in case of | instead of |
| by way of | in lieu of | on account of |
| in care of | in spite of | on the side of |

*In care of* is a common symbol used in correspondence.   (*In care of* is a phrasal preposition that serves as the subject of the verb *is.*)

They traveled **by way of** Vermont.   (The phrasal preposition *by way of* modifies the verb *traveled.* The noun *Vermont* is the object of the phrase.)

## Common Errors to Avoid

Prepositions are among the most overworked words in the English language. Use the following guidelines to avoid committing two of the more common errors.

### 1. Avoid putting unnecessary prepositions at the end of sentences.

| | |
|---|---|
| *Incorrect:* | Where are the boys **at?** |
| *Correct:* | Where are the boys? |
| *Incorrect:* | Can I go **with?** |
| *Correct:* | Can I go? or Can I go **with you?** |
| *Incorrect:* | Where did that cat get **to?** |
| *Correct:* | Where is that cat? |

### 2. In formal writing and business communications, avoid putting the preposition at the end of a sentence. Rewrite the sentence so that it has a correct prepositional phrase.

| | |
|---|---|
| *Avoid:* | They were not sure which city they were going **to.** |
| *Better:* | They were not sure **to** which city they were going.   (The preposition is now part of the phrase *to which city.*) |
| *Avoid:* | Ask not whom the bell tolls **for.** |
| *Better:* | Ask not **for whom** the bell tolls. |

## Prepositions Used with Verbs

These guidelines are not rigid. Winston Churchill once remarked, "This is the sort of English up with which I will not put."

Obviously, there will be exceptions to the rule, particularly when prepositions are used with verbs. In the quote above, the verb-preposition form is *to put up with.* In writing, however, it is best to recast the sentence to read "I will not put up with this sort of English."

Prepositions are used with verbs to change the meaning slightly or to distinguish between people and objects. For example:

Accompany by (a person)

Accompany with (an object)

The president was **accompanied by** his wife.

The letter was **accompanied with** a postage-due notice.

Knowing when to use the right preposition with a verb can be a challenge. Some of the most commonly confused verb-preposition combinations are listed in Appendix B on page 127.

# Conjunctions

*Conjunctions* link words or groups of words to other parts of the sentence and show the relationship between them. The four basic conjunctions are coordinating, correlative, subordinating conjunctions, and linking adverbs.

## Coordinating Conjunctions

Coordinating conjunctions *and, but, or,* and *nor* join two or more elements of equal rank. The conjunctions *but* and *nor* often are used with the adverbs *never* or *not*.

The elements joined by coordinating conjunctions can be single words—nouns, verbs, adjectives, adverbs, pronouns—or phrases or clauses. (Clauses are groups of words with a subject-verb combination such as *when she came to work* or *because they are sailing tomorrow.*)

> The starship **and** its shuttle were repaired.   (nouns)
>
> We have tried **and** tried to warn him.   (verbs)
>
> He is a sore **but** jubilant player tonight.   (adjectives)
>
> You can have it done quickly **or** thoroughly.   (adverbs)
>
> She **and** I seldom agree on anything.   (pronouns)
>
> We can go over the river **or** through the woods.   (prepositional phrases)
>
> Did you know that he's **never** eaten a hot dog, had a real root beer, **nor** played miniature golf?   (verb phrases)
>
> She went home last night **and** found the jury summons waiting for her.   (clauses)

## Correlative Conjunctions

*Correlative conjunctions* are coordinating conjunctions used in pairs, and they emphasize the elements being joined. Some of the most frequently used correlative conjunctions are as follows:

> both . . . and
> either . . . or
> neither . . . nor
> not only . . . but also

Correlative conjunctions also join elements of *equal rank*. Make sure that the elements following each part of the construction are truly equal.

Don't let **either** Judith **or** Andy know we have money.   (nouns)

It is **both** raining **and** snowing outside.   (verb forms)

The contract negotiations were **neither** hostile **nor** overly friendly.   (adjectives)

He **not only** has ordered a large pizza **but also** has given me the check!   (verb phrases)

## Subordinating Conjunctions

Unlike the conjunctions described in the preceding section, *subordinating conjunctions* join elements of *unequal rank* in a sentence. These elements are usually a subordinate clause (a group of words with a subject-verb combination that cannot stand alone) and an independent clause. Following is a list of commonly used subordinating conjunctions.

| | | | |
|---|---|---|---|
| after | how | than | when |
| although | if | that | where |
| as | in order that | though | which |
| as much as | inasmuch as | unless | while |
| because | provided | until | who/whom |
| before | since | what | whoever/ whomever |

Subordinating conjunctions can be used to introduce a sentence as well as to join elements within it. When a subordinate clause comes at the beginning of a sentence, it is followed by a comma. No comma is used when the subordinate clause comes at the end of the sentence.

**Before** we left the theater, I had to dry my eyes.
I had to dry my eyes **before** we left the theater.

**Provided** the books arrive, we can start class Tuesday.
We can start class Tuesday **provided** the books arrive.

**Restrictive and Nonrestrictive Clauses**   Some clauses provide additional information about a person, place, or object within a sentence. When the clause is essential to the meaning of that sentence, it is known as a *restrictive clause*. When it is descriptive but not essential, it is called a *nonrestrictive clause*.

*Restrictive:*  The city **that was built along the river** escaped the fire. (The clause *that was built along the river* distinguishes this city from all others in the area. The information is essential to the sentence.)

*Nonrestrictive:*  The city, **which was built along the river,** escaped the fire. (In this sentence, the clause *which was built along the river* is simply descriptive information.)

Notice that the subordinating conjunction changes from *that* in a restrictive clause to *which* in a nonrestrictive clause. In general, *that* is used to indicate information essential to the meaning of the sentence. *Which* indicates information that is not essential.

To decide whether a clause is restrictive or nonrestrictive, eliminate the clause from the sentence and determine if doing so changes the meaning.

> The secretary **who works for John** has been absent lately.
>
> The secretary, **who works for John,** has been absent lately.

In the first sentence, *who works for John* identifies which secretary among several is missing. The second sentence implies that the *secretary*, as opposed to the accountant or some other individual, has been absent. The information *who works for John* can be eliminated without changing the meaning of the sentence.

## Linking Adverbs

*Linking adverbs* are used to join two *independent clauses,* that is, clauses with a subject-verb combination that can stand alone. Linking adverbs indicate the relationship between two ideas expressed in independent clauses. In general, linking adverbs reflect results, contrast, or continuation.

| *Results* | *Contrast* | *Continuation* |
|---|---|---|
| accordingly | nevertheless | furthermore |
| as a result | however | further |
| therefore | nonetheless | in addition |
| thus | conversely | also |

Linking adverbs can come at the beginning of the second clause they are joining. In such cases, they are usually preceded by a semicolon and followed by a comma. They also can stand within the second clause or sentence and often are set off by commas.

> We arrived late at night; **however,** the motel was still open.
>
> I fail to see your point; **furthermore,** your entire argument is off the subject.
>
> The strike delayed shipment; **therefore,** your order will not be sent on the date we promised.
>
> The train slipped off the track at Innesbruck; the passengers, **accordingly,** had to continue by taxis.
>
> The storm ruined two speakers; the band, **however,** had spare ones in their van.

# Interjections

*Interjections* are words used to express emotion or to catch the reader's attention. Interjections are rarely used in formal or business writing but do appear in advertising and promotional material, fiction, informal writing, and personal letters.

## Common Interjections

Some of the most commonly used interjections are listed below.

| | | |
|---|---|---|
| ah | hey | no way |
| alas | hooray | oh |
| congratulations | hurry | ouch |
| good grief | my goodness | outstanding |
| great | never | ugh |
| help | no | wow |

## Punctuation

Strong interjections are punctuated with an exclamation point (*wow! ouch! hooray!*). The first word following the exclamation point is capitalized since it is the first word in a new sentence.

Milder interjections are set off by commas and often introduce a sentence (*indeed, yes, well*). The word following the comma is not capitalized because it is a continuation of the same sentence.

*Strong interjections:* **Excellent!** That was a perfect dive.
You may be saying, "**Hey!** Why is the coffee cold?"

*Mild interjections:* **No,** we can't visit you this summer.
**Well,** I just thought I'd ask.

# 1.2 Punctuation and Punctuation Style

Punctuation serves two important purposes in written communication. First, it helps present ideas clearly and accurately. It indicates where one thought ends and another begins, shows relationships among ideas, and separates items in a series. Second, punctuation is used in abbreviations and in figures expressing time, quantities, and measures.

This section covers proper usage of end marks, commas, semicolons, colons, apostrophes, hyphens, dashes, brackets, parentheses, and ellipses.

## End Marks—Period, Question Mark, Exclamation Point

*End marks* usually come at the end of a sentence. However, they also can be used after single words or within a sentence.

### Period

The *period* is used at the end of a complete sentence, which can be a statement, command, or request. It is a visual marker to the reader that one complete thought has ended and that another may follow. In informal writing, periods can be used with single words.

|  |  |
|---|---|
| *Statement:* | Your bicycle is on my foot. |
| *Request:* | Please move your bicycle off my foot. |
| *Command:* | Get your bicycle off my foot. |
| *Single words:* | Thanks. That feels much better. |

Periods are also used in many abbreviations. For a more complete discussion of abbreviations, see pages 64-73.

|  |  |
|---|---|
| Saint | St. |
| Cash on delivery | C.O.D. |
| Avenue | Ave. |
| Youth Umbrella Organization | Y.U.O. |

## Question Mark

A *question mark* is used at the end of a sentence that asks a direct question. It is not used at the end of a statement that contains an *indirect* question. In informal writing, question marks also can be used with single words.

| | |
|---|---|
| *Direct question:* | Are you going to the fiesta tonight? |
| *Indirect question:* | I asked them if they were going to the fiesta tonight. |
| *Single words:* | What? I couldn't hear you over the radio. |
| | So? It's no trouble to make room for another guest. |

**Polite Requests**   Many business letters contain requests for information, compliance, reply, or permission. These requests can be punctuated using either a period or a question mark.

| | |
|---|---|
| *Period:* | Would you please send me a brochure describing your company's products. |
| *Question mark:* | Would you please send me a brochure describing your company's products? |

**Series of Questions**   Question marks are used after each question in a sentence containing a series of questions.

How much are you willing to gamble on your future? your family's health? your career?

**Quotation Marks**   Question marks are placed *inside* quotation marks when the quoted material is a question. Otherwise, they are placed *outside* quotation marks.

"Are the stuntmen in place?" the director asked.

I just finished the short story "Where Are We Going?"

Have you read "Ballad of the Sad Cafe"? (The quoted material is not a question. The entire sentence is the question.)

Did he say "no vacation" or "no early vacation"?

## Exclamation Point

*Exclamation points* add emphasis to sentences, phrases, or single words. They are like a red flag waved at the reader and as such should be used sparingly. Exclamation points are a familiar sight in advertising and promotional material.

"Wait! Don't touch that wire!"

"I can't believe she said that!"

Don't delay! Order your album now!

# Comma

The *comma* is the most commonly used and abused punctuation mark. People often insert commas between subject and verb or when they reach the end of a thought, without regard for the rules of comma usage.

Commas are used to separate words or groups of words in a list or parallel construction; to set off introductory elements, interruptions, and words moved from their usual positon; and to coordinate such grammatical structures as compound predicates, coordinate adjectives, and descriptive appositives and modifiers. On the other hand, some comma uses have little to do with the meaning of a sentence and are inserted to prevent misreading or to create emphasis. In a few cases, they simply represent traditional ways of punctuating various grammatical elements.

This section discusses some of the more common uses and abuses of this often troublesome punctuation mark.

## Series Commas

Commas separate items in a series. The items can be single words, phrases, or clauses. Although current practice allows the final comma to be dropped before the final conjunction (*or, but, nor,* and *and*), including the comma can avoid possible confusion for the reader.

> We brought sandwiches, wine, cold soup, and chocolate cake on the picnic.
>
> The conductor set up his stand, took out the score, and lifted his baton.   (verb phrases)
>
> She is vice president of operations, sales and resources and personnel.   (Are the final categories *sales and resources,* and *personnel* or are they *sales,* and *resources and personnel*? A final comma would make the categories clear.)

## Independent Clauses

When two independent clauses are joined by *and, but, or, nor,* or *for,* use a comma before the conjunction. However, no comma is needed if the clauses are very short.

> Her performance was brilliant, and the judges awarded her four perfect tens.
>
> Yolanda knew we'd be late, but she left anyway.
>
> He can play the guitar, or he can do his magic show.
>
> Stir the batter and add the eggs slowly.
>
> They came early and they left late.

A comma is not used when *and, but, for, or,* or *nor* joins two verbs that share the same subject.

> Greg Maddux **pitches** with the best of them and **bats** better than most outfielders.
>
> Shelly **hasn't driven** in the city nor **ridden** on the subway.

## Introductory Clauses, Phrases, Expressions

Use a comma after introductory phrases or clauses unless they are very short. When expressions such as *no, yes, in addition, well,* and *thus* begin a sentence, they are followed by a comma.

When Ansel Adams took a photograph, he knew exactly what would appear in the picture.

Speaking of food, isn't anybody hungry?

In summer we always move to the country. (Short phrase "in summer" does not require a comma.)

Well, losing one game doesn't ruin an entire season.

Thus, I feel your qualifications make you perfectly suited for this job.

## Nonrestrictive Clauses and Nonessential Material

Commas set off nonrestrictive clauses and expressions that interrupt the sentence or that add incidental information or description.

The rodeo, held in August, always drew a large tourist crowd. (*Held in August* is a nonrestrictive clause.)

We wanted to finish, of course, before night fell.

The new officer, I'm sure you remember him, stopped by the house yesterday and left your orders.

## Direct Address

Words used in direct address are set off by commas regardless of their position in the sentence.

Greg, can you lift this chair?

They heard about the trouble, Jean, and wanted to help.

Please sign this receipt, Ms. Liang.

## Commas and Clarity

At times commas are used to avoid confusing the reader when a sentence can be read in more than one way.

In autumn nights grow steadily longer. (On first reading, *autumn* and *nights* appear to go together. It's evident from the rest of the sentence, however, that they are separate. A comma after *autumn* would make the meaning clear.)

In autumn, nights grow steadily longer.

## Traditional Comma Uses

Commas are used in certain conventional situations including dates, addresses, the salutations and closings of informal letters, and certain forms of proper names or names followed by a title.

> We were married June 22, 1941, in Los Angeles. (When only the day and month are used, no commas are necessary: *We were married on June 22 in Los Angeles.*)
>
> Send $4.00 and a self-addressed, stamped envelope to Harvard House, Suite 2920, 467 West Rhine Street, Portland, Oregon.
>
> Dear Harriet,   Sincerely yours,   Truly yours,
>
> Samuel Stanislaw, Jr.   (But *Samuel Stanislaw III*)
>
> Judith Gallagher, Ph.D.   Linda Marks, director

## Comma Faults

Many people use commas incorrectly. The following guidelines point out common errors in style.

### 1. Never use commas to separate subject and verb.

> *Incorrect:* Dealing with the lead singer in the band, has been an ordeal. (The noun phrase *Dealing with the lead singer in the band* is the subject and should not be separated from the verb *has been.*)
>
> *Correct:* Dealing with the lead singer in the band has been an ordeal.

### 2. Never use commas to separate two phrases or subordinate clauses joined by a conjunction.

> *Incorrect:* The waiter suggested that we order a white wine, and that we try the Cajun appetizers.
>
> *Correct:* The waiter suggested that we order a white wine and that we try the Cajun appetizers.
>
> *Incorrect:* Howard painted the steps, but not the porch.
>
> *Correct:* Howard painted the steps but not the porch.
>
> *Incorrect:* After the treaty was signed, both sides pulled back their troops, and reduced their armored divisions.
>
> *Correct:* After the treaty was signed, both sides pulled back their troops and reduced their armored divisions.

**3. In a series, never use a comma to separate a modifier from the word it modifies.**

| | |
|---|---|
| *Incorrect:* | They drove through a damp, cold, eerie, fog. |
| *Correct:* | They drove through a damp, cold, eerie fog. |
| *Incorrect:* | That is a ridiculous, immature, wicked, suggestion. |
| *Correct:* | That is a ridiculous, immature, wicked suggestion. |

# Semicolon

A *semicolon* represents a stronger break than a comma but not as complete a stop as a period or colon. Semicolons are used to separate independent clauses in a variety of special circumstances. They also serve to group items in a series when the items contain internal punctuation.

## Independent Clauses

Use a semicolon to join two independent clauses that are similar in thought but are *not* joined by a coordinating conjunction *and, but, or, nor, for,* or *yet.*

The house stood empty for years; no one would buy it.

The river raged through the gorge; her small tent was swept away in its path.

**Joined by Linking Adverb**  When two independent clauses are joined by a linking adverb such as *accordingly, however, therefore,* or *thus,* use a semicolon at the end of the first clause. The linking adverb is usually followed by a comma or set off by commas if it falls within the second clause.

The turtle survived its two-story fall; however, it was never quite the same again.

The conference ended last Thursday; therefore, we can get back to business on Monday.

Margaret told me not to stay in a motel; she suggested, instead, that I stay at her house.

**Clauses with Internal Punctuation**  A semicolon is used to separate two independent clauses if one or both of the clauses contain internal punctuation. The clauses may or may not be joined by conjunctions or linking adverbs.

I own a quarter horse, a saddle horse, and a burro; they stay on the lower range in winter.

Walter, the one with the allergies, read his story in class; and everyone thought it was excellent.

The dark, dusty street looked deserted; but I could hear someone walking slowly behind me.

## Series

Use semicolons to separate items in a series if the items contain internal punctuation.

> The speakers included Jeff Hines, vice president; Alberta Corazon, director of finances; Edward Singh, human resources; and Nancy Meripol, assistant to the president.
>
> We ordered five cartons of micro-perf paper; six lined, medium-sized stationery pads; and nine boxes of assorted pens, pencils, and markers.

# Colon

*Colons* represent a more complete break than semicolons but not as complete a stop as a period. Like the period, a colon is followed by two full spaces in typed or printed communication.

## Before a Series or List

Colons are used to introduce a series or list only after a complete sentence. When the series immediately follows a verb or preposition, do not use a colon.

> *Incorrect:* Our five travel choices are: the Bahamas, Hawaii, Mexico City, Acapulco, and Peoria.
>
> *Correct:* We have five travel choices: the Bahamas, Hawaii, Mexico City, Acapulco, and Peoria.
>
> *Incorrect:* They were interested in: one brass bed, two lace pillows, one afghan comforter, and a chamber pot.
>
> *Correct:* They were interested in the following items: one brass bed, two lace pillows, one afghan comforter, and a chamber pot.

## Between Independent Clauses

Use a colon to introduce a question or related statement following an independent clause. The second independent clause may or may not begin with a capital letter.

> She had only one thought: What was she going to do now?
>
> I know the answer: reverse the two equations.

## Time

Colons are used to express time in figures. Do not use the words *o'clock* after the figures. However, expressions such as *noon, in the afternoon, A.M., P.M.,* and *midnight* can be used.

| | |
|---|---|
| 10:30 A.M. | 4:35 P.M. |
| 12:00 midnight | 8:30 in the morning |

## Formal and Business Communications

Colons follow the salutation in a formal or business letter, report, memo, or other type of business communication.

| | |
|---|---|
| Dear Mr. Winfield: | To the Research Staff: |
| Dear Buyer: | To All Managers: |
| Dear President West: | Attention Union Members: |

# Quotation Marks

*Quotation marks* enclose a direct quotation, that is, the repetition of someone's exact words.

"Keep your head down and charge!" the coach said.

Her exact words were "Bake the bread at 350 degrees."

Indirect quotations do not take quotation marks.

The coach said to keep your head down and charge.

She told us to bake the bread at 350 degrees.

## Punctuation with Quotation Marks

Commas and periods are always placed *inside* the closing quote marks even if the quoted material is contained within the sentence.

She thinks we're "off the wall," but I think our idea will work.

We've heard him say a thousand times, "Waste not, want not."

"Tell me something I'll remember forever," she said.

You've read the poem "Ash Wednesday," haven't you?

Semicolons and colons are always placed *outside* the quotation marks.

Look up the title under "Animated Cartoons"; copy the cartoon features listed there.

The following animals are considered "marsupials": kangaroo, wombat, and koala.

Question marks and exclamation points are placed *inside* the final quotation mark if they are part of the quoted material. Otherwise they are placed *outside* the quotation marks. Only one end mark is used at the end of a sentence containing quoted material.

Have you read the report "Single-Parent Families"? (The entire sentence is the question; the end mark comes after the final quotation mark.)

He sent Josh the article "Why Can't Ivan Compute?" (The title is a question and the end mark comes before the final quotation marks.)

"Dinner is hot and ready to eat!" he called.

I can't believe they want us to increase sales "by twenty percent"!

## Brief and Long Quotations

Quoted material that is only two or three lines long is enclosed in quotation marks and included as part of the regular text.

> The movie critic was blunt about her reactions to the film. She stated that it **"has the intelligence of a jellyfish and as much reality as Max Klinger's insanity pleas."**

Longer quotations have no quote marks and are set off from the rest of the text by being indented and single spaced.

> The movie critic was blunt about her reactions to the film.
>
> > **This movie should suffer an early and merciful death. It has the intelligence of a jellyfish and as much reality as Max Klinger's insanity pleas. I don't know what the director intended for this film; but unless it was to bore us to death, he has certainly failed.**

## Single Quotation Marks

*Single quotation marks* are used to set off a quote within a quote.

> Carla said, "Every time I hear 'Amazing Grace' I want to cry."
>
> "When I asked him what he wanted, he replied, 'Safe passage to Cairo.'"

## Titles

Quotation marks are used to enclose the titles of articles, chapters of books, poems, reports, many government publications, short stories, individual songs, workshop or conference titles, and titles of proceedings.

> "The Snows of Kilimanjaro" is required reading in most college literature programs.
>
> "Born in the USA" made Bruce Springsteen as well known as Tina Turner.
>
> Read the chapter "How Diet Affects Immune Functions" before you change your eating habits too radically.
>
> The report "Equality in the Workplace: A Ten-year Study" shows how much work still needs to be done.
>
> Louise Glück's poem "The Triumph of Achilles" appears in her latest collection.
>
> The IEEE international conference focused on the theme "Ultrasonic Research: Practical Applications."
>
> Throughout the weekend, we will offer two workshops titled "Living with Stress" and "Getting Control of Your Finances."

## Terms and Expressions

Use quotation marks to enclose terms and expressions that are considered odd or unusual (slang terms in a formal report) or that are likely to be unknown to the reader (jargon, technical terms).

The President told reporters he regarded his opponents as "flaky."

Not many people know the functions of "T cells" or "B cells" in the immune system.

Scott said he was as full as "a bug-eyed tick."

The term "downloaded" should be defined in your book.

# Apostrophe

The *apostrophe* is used to show possession and to form the plural of many nouns and symbols. (Possessive nouns and pronouns are also covered in Parts of Speech under Nouns and Pronouns on pages 4 and 6.)

## Possessive of Singular Nouns

The possessive of a singular noun is formed by adding *'s*. Names that end in a *z* sound often take only the apostrophe to avoid the awkwardness of too many *s* sounds.

| | |
|---|---|
| the **mechanic's** wrench | **Gloria's** briefcase |
| the **tree's** leaves | Mr. **Jones'** house |
| **Moses'** tablets | **Gus's** workbench |
| Mrs. **Gonzales'** maid | Ned **Stanis's** boots |

## Possessive of Plural Nouns

The plural possessive of nouns ending in *s* is formed by adding only the apostrophe. All other plural nouns take *'s*.

| | |
|---|---|
| the **Harlands'** trip | the **trees'** leaves |
| **children's** shoes | **men's** sports wear |
| the **teams'** scores | **women's** networks |

## Indefinite and Personal Pronouns

Indefinite pronouns (*everyone, no one, anybody, everybody, someone, somebody, one*) require an apostrophe to form the possessive. However, personal possessive pronouns (*his, hers, theirs, your/yours, my/mine, our/ours*) do not use an apostrophe.

| | |
|---|---|
| Is this **someone's** book? | Yes, the book is **hers.** |
| I'll take **anyone's** ideas. | **Your** ideas are great. |

## Individual and Joint Possession

When hyphenated words or names of organizations, companies, or individuals are used to show *joint possession,* only the last word takes *'s* or an apostrophe.

  In cases of *individual possession,* both nouns or pronouns take *'s* or the apostrophe only.

| | |
|---|---|
| *Joint possession:* | **Lin and Chan's** bicycle   (The bicycle is owned by both Lin and Chan.) |
| | the **vice-presidents'** office   (The office is used by more than one vice president.) |
| | **IBM and Xerox's** new venture   (The two companies are working together on one venture.) |
| *Individual possession:* | **Lin's** and **Chan's** bicycles   (Notice the plural noun after the names—a clue that each person owns a bicycle.) |
| | her **father-in-law's** and **brother's** golf scores |
| | **Texaco's** and **Esso's** annual reports |

## Units of Measure as Possessive Adjectives

Units of measure such as *day, week, yard, cent,* and *hour* take an *'s* or an apostrophe when used as possessive adjectives.

a **moment's** peace          ten **minutes'** work
a **month's** pay            three **weeks'** pay
a **dollar's** worth          two **cents'** worth

## Plural Forms of Symbols

The apostrophe or *'s* is used to form the plural of letters, numbers, signs, symbols, and words referred to as words.

All the **R's** in this article were printed backwards.
Mark these items with **X's** and those with **Z's**.
Your **3's** look like **8's**.
How many **and's** can you put in one sentence?
My typewriter smudged all the **&'s** in my letter.

# Hyphens

Hyphens are used to join two or more words that are used as a single unit, to link two last names, to join continuous numbers, to connect some prefixes and suffixes with their nouns, to divide words at the end of a line, and to avoid confusing or awkward word constructions.

## Compound Numbers and Fractions

Hyphens are used with compound numbers from twenty-one to ninety-nine and with fractions used as adjectives. However, when fractions serve as nouns, no hyphen is used.

**twenty-one** red roses
**sixty-five** and over

a **two-thirds** majority
a glass **three-fifths** full
*But:* two tenths of a percent (*Two tenths* is used as a noun.)

## Continuous Numbers

Hyphens are used to link dates of birth and death, pages of material, scores of games, and other instances in which the relationship between the numbers needs to be shown.

T. E. Lawrence, "Lawrence of Arabia," (**1888–1935**)

Read pages **15–32** in your statistics book.

The Bears beat the Rams **21–0.**

All children ages **8–12** are eligible for camp.

## Prefixes and Suffixes

Prefixes *ex-, self-, all-* and the suffix *-elect* always take a hyphen whether they are used as modifiers or as nouns. Hyphens also are used with all prefixes before proper nouns and adjectives.

**self-esteem**
**ex-director**

**secretary-elect**
**all-encompassing**

**all-Canadian team**
**pro-French**

## Compound Adjectives

When compound adjectives are used before the noun, they are hyphenated. When they follow the noun, no hyphen is used. If one of the modifiers is an adverb ending in *-ly,* do not use a hyphen in the compound adjective.

a **decision-making** process
a **well-run** program
a **city-owned** business
**publicly owned** parks

a process for **decision making**
a program that is **well run**
a business that is **city owned**
parks that are **publicly owned**

## Word Division

Hyphens are used to divide words at the end of a line as a reminder that the rest of the word is to follow. Words cannot be divided arbitrarily but only between syllables. See the section on Word Division, pages 96-98, for rules on dividing words at the end of a line.

> We were almost in Niles **Town-**
> **ship** when our car broke down.
> Sam didn't really want to **con-**
> **tinue** the trip, but I did.

## Hyphenated Names

Hyphens are used to join two last names.

Karen **Norridge-Adams**                Mr. Michael **Harrington-Kelly**
the **Henderson-Smythes**               Mr. and Mrs. **Barry-Schroeder**

## To Avoid Confusion

Use hyphens to prevent confusion or awkwardness in sentences.

**re-creation**   (prevents confusion with *recreation*)
**re-emphasize**   (avoids awkwardness of *reemphasize*)
**sub-subentry**   (avoids confusion of *subsubentry*)

# Dashes

A *dash* indicates a break in thought or the addition of information within a sentence or at its end. A dash is typed using two hyphens. There is no space before or after the punctuation mark.

> The woman came running around the corner — I couldn't see her face — and disappeared down the alley.
> This building — and every building on the street — is overdue for repairs.
> Paul White — you know the man I mean — told me the ballgame would be canceled tomorrow.

A dash can be used to mean *namely, that is,* or *in other words* to introduce additional information or an explanation.

> I thought about taking another route — the one through West Virginia.
> There's only one way to ride that horse — take out a lot of accident insurance.

# Parentheses

*Parentheses* ( ) enclose material that is an interruption of the text but adds information.

The park (in Washington) is always crowded in summer.
I know the answer (I think) to the final question.

If the material enclosed falls at the end of a sentence, the end mark is placed *outside* the closing parenthesis. If the material is a complete sentence within itself, the end mark is placed *inside* the parenthesis.

We provide a complete list of stores (see the Appendix).
We provide a complete list of stores. (See the Appendix.)

# Brackets

Use *brackets* to enclose additions to quoted material. These additions, made by editors or writers, usually clarify or comment on the material.

"Mark Twain said it [the river] taught him all he ever knew about life."
"Virginia Woolf lived with him [Lytton Strachey] while recovering from her illness."
"There were few Esquimouxs [sic] living in the region we explored."

Brackets are also used to enclose material that falls within material already enclosed by parentheses.

The fall sales records are encouraging (see page 33, Monthly Sales [Table 2.1] for a detailed breakdown by product line).

# Ellipses

*Ellipses* points (. . .) indicate that material has been omitted from a quotation or quoted material.

|  |  |
|---|---|
| *Original:* | This book describes the author's visit to Nepal and renders scenes of the rugged, mountainous countryside that will remain in the reader's mind forever. |
| *Condensed:* | This book . . . renders scenes . . . that will remain in the reader's mind forever. |

When words are omitted at the end of a sentence, use an end mark plus the ellipses.

This book . . . renders scenes of the rugged, mountainous countryside. . . .

# Italics

*Italics* are used to indicate emphasis, to mark foreign terms and expressions not commonly used, and to highlight titles of publications and names of certain vehicles such as ships, spacecraft, and the like. Use the underscore for any item that would be italicized in print.

## Emphasis

Occasionally, italics are used to stress certain words or phrases. This usage is more common in dialogue than in formal writing and should be kept to a minimum.

> "I didn't want *blue* paint; I wanted *lavender* paint!"
>
> "Mr. Lloyd, you told the prosecutor that you didn't meet Mrs. Young *until last month*, is that right?"
>
> On the basis of the field inspector's report, I recommend that *we shut down offshore drilling platform #45*.

## Foreign Words and Phrases

Foreign words and phrases that are not part of common usage are italicized.

> The motto of the Coast Guard is *semper paratus*—always prepared.
>
> As they say, *Ende gut, alles gut*: all's well that ends well.

However, many foreign words have been in common use long enough that they are no longer italicized.

> His clothes are very **avant-garde**.
>
> At one time the motto **caveat emptor**—let the buyer beware—was the rule in business.
>
> Her hat is **chic**, her shoes **passé**.
>
> The military **junta** declared a 7:00 P.M. curfew.

## Titles

The titles of plays, books, magazines, newspapers, movies, and other types of periodicals and publications are italicized when they appear in print. If the first word of a title is *a, an,* or *the,* it is italicized only if it is part of the actual name.

| | |
|---|---|
| *The Wall Street Journal* (newspaper) | *Esquire* (magazine) |
| the *Los Angeles Times* (newspaper) | *The Color Purple* (movie) |
| *Chorus Line* (play) | *Redbook* (magazine) |
| *The Insider* (corporate publication) | *The Yearling* (book) |
| *Editorial Eye* (newsletter) | |

## Vehicles

Use italics for the names of ships, spacecraft, airplanes, and other well-known vehicles.

the battleship *Excalibur*

the spaceship *Enterprise*

the *Titanic*

the president's jet *Air Force One*

# 1.3 Sentences and Sentence Patterns

The English language provides considerable flexibility in sentence construction. Using various sentence patterns produces speech and writing that are lively and interesting. Also, variety in sentence construction contributes to well-organized messages. (See pages 101-4 for more on sentence patterns.)

This section explains the building blocks of sentences—phrases and clauses, subjects and predicates—and the various ways sentences are constructed.

## Sentences, Fragments, and Run-ons

A *sentence* is a group of words that expresses a complete thought. It begins with a capital letter and closes with an end mark, either a period, a question mark, or an exclamation mark. Sentences are classified as declarative (a statement), interrogative (a question), imperative (command or request), or exclamatory (for emphasis).

| | |
|---|---|
| *Declarative:* | The waffles are almost ready. |
| *Interrogative:* | What did the doctor say when you saw her? |
| *Imperative:* | Please hand me the butter. Go to your room. |
| *Exclamatory:* | I just got Yo-Yo Ma's autograph! |

Not every group of words is a sentence. A *fragment* is a phrase or clause that looks like a sentence but does not express a complete thought.

| | |
|---|---|
| *Fragment:* | Down by the river where the fish bite. |
| | If he would just think. |

By themselves, fragments make little sense and leave important questions unanswered. What would happen *if he would just think*? Who or what is *down by the river where the fish bite*? Fragments must be joined with other sentence parts to form a complete thought.

| | |
|---|---|
| *Sentence:* | **We were** down by the river where the fish bite. |
| | **He could save himself so much trouble** if he would just think. |

Unlike fragments, which haven't enough parts to make a complete sentence, *run-ons* have too many parts. They are two or more complete thoughts—at times only vaguely related—strung together without punctuation.

> *Run-on:* We have only three days until the band contest I don't have my uniform repaired yet and that will take at least a day or so to do, don't you think?

Run-on sentences can be corrected in a number of ways: by inserting the proper punctuation, by breaking the sentence into two or more smaller sentences, or by rewriting the sentence to eliminate the run-on.

> *Revised:* We have only three days until the band contest, and I forgot to have my uniform repaired. Do you think the repairs will take more than a day or so?
>
> We have only three days to practice until the band contest. I forgot to have my uniform repaired. Do you think the repairs will take more than a day or so?

# Phrases and Clauses

The various parts of speech are grouped into phrases and clauses which make up the basic sentence.

## Phrases

*Phrases* are groups of related words that do not contain a subject-verb combination or express a complete thought. There are noun, prepositional, participial, verb, and infinitive phrases.

| | | |
|---|---|---|
| *Noun:* | my brand new car | the sad old horse |
| *Prepositional:* | over the wall | around the block |
| *Participial:* | playing the fool | buying the book |
| *Verb:* | will be given | is coming |
| *Infinitive:* | to think | to draw |

## Clauses

*Clauses* are groups of related words that contain a subject-verb combination. *Independent clauses* express a complete thought and can stand by themselves as sentences. *Subordinate clauses* serve as part of a sentence but do not express a complete thought and cannot stand by themselves. They are subordinate to independent clauses.

> *Independent clauses:* the weather was warm and dry
>
> John got free tickets to the play
>
> they took the wrong road

|   |   |
|---|---|
| *Subordinate clauses:* | by the time June arrived |
|   | because he works at the theater |
|   | when they came to the turn |
| *Complete sentences:* | **By the time June arrived,** the weather was warm and dry. |
|   | John got free tickets to the play, **because he works at the theater.** |
|   | **When they came to the turn,** they took the wrong road. |

# Subject and Predicate

The *subject* is the topic of the sentence. The *predicate* is what is said about the subject.

| Subject | Predicate |
|---|---|
| The balloon | floated up through the trees. |
| New York City | is a major cultural center. |
| The lion tamer | astonished the audience. |

In most cases, as in the preceding examples, the subject of a sentence comes first, followed by the predicate. However, there are instances when the subject is placed after the predicate, omitted from the sentence, or placed inside the verb.

Into the valley of death rode **the six hundred.**

Wash the car by tonight.   (subject *you* is understood)

Are **your parents** coming tomorrow?

There are **four chickens** in the yard.   (*There* occupies the place of the subject, but *four chickens* is still the subject of the sentence.)

## Forms of the Subject

The most common forms of the subject are nouns, pronouns, and proper nouns.

**Carol** came close to flunking her classes this year.

Why don't **you** pick up some lettuce for tonight?

**Who** left these socks here?

At times, noun phrases and clauses, gerunds and gerund phrases, and infinitive phrases can also function as the subject.

| | |
|---|---|
| *Noun phrase:* | **The girl on the swing** is my niece. |
| *Noun clause:* | **What they said** upset Francine. |
| *Gerund:* | **Swimming** is my favorite sport. |
| *Gerund phrase:* | **Playing checkers** kept him from thinking about his injuries. |
| *Infinitive phrase:* | **To see clearly** is an artist's greatest task. |

**Complete Subject**   The noun or pronoun and all its modifiers are known as the *complete subject*.

> **The ship in the harbor** seemed small and frail.
>
> **What he said in the car** surprised us all.
>
> **The trees, which had been damaged in the storm,** were cut down the next day and burned.

**Simple and Compound Subjects**   The noun or pronoun by itself is known as the *simple subject*. It is important to identify the subject because it controls the form of the verb used in the sentence.

> The **ship** in the harbor seemed small and frail.
>
> **Daffodils** open in early spring.
>
> **They** reported the fire immediately.

The *compound subject* is composed of two or more nouns, pronouns, or phrases or clauses to express the topic of a sentence.

|  |  |
|---|---|
| *Nouns:* | The **wheat** and **oats** ripened late this year. |
| *Pronouns:* | **She** and **I** used to be best friends in high school. |
| *Noun clauses:* | **What he wanted** and **what he got** were two different things. |
| *Gerund phrases:* | **Hiking in the mountains** and **camping out at night** are experiences everyone should enjoy. |

# Forms of the Predicate

The predicate always contains a verb. An action verb generally will have an object as well as various verb modifiers. A linking verb will have a complement along with its verb modifiers.

Thus, the predicate usually is composed of a verb, object or complement, and verb modifiers.

**Predicate with Action Verbs**   The most common form of predicate is one in which the verb describes some sort of action. The verb is followed by a direct object (d.o.) and, in some cases, by an indirect object (ind.o.).

> d.o.        ind.o.
> Indiana Jones threw the **jewel** to his **partner.**
>
> d.o.              d.o.
> I brought four **sandwiches** and one **pizza.**
>
> d.o.
> Carl Lewis won four gold **medals** in the Olympics.
>
> d.o.     ind.o.
> She called a **cab** for **him.**

Some action verbs can drop their objects and still make sense. The predicate then consists of the verb only.

> They **have been practicing.**
> We **were reading.**
> The reporter **disappeared.**
> The weather **has changed.**

Action verbs can also take complements. Nouns, pronouns, prepositional phrases, adjectives, and verb phrases can serve as complements in the predicate.

> He taught the dog **to roll over.**   (The infinitive phrase *to roll over* is the complement.)
> I called him a **prince.**   (The noun *prince* is the complement.)
> They made camp **on the hill.**   (The prepositional phrase *on the hill* is the complement.)
> Her pony behaved **beautifully.**   (The adverb *beautifully* is the complement.)
> We saw the tornado **heading this way.**   (The participial phrase *heading this way* is the complement.)
> She lay **down in the tall grass.**   (The adverb *down* and the prepositional phrase *in the tall grass* are the complement and indicate direction and location.)

**Predicate with Linking Verbs**   Linking verbs that express being, seeming, or becoming need a predicate or verb complement to complete them. The more common of these verbs include *seem, become, grow, taste, smell, appear, look, feel,* and *sound.*

> He looks **sick.**   (*He looks* is incomplete. The adjective *sick* acts as the predicate complement.)
> I feel **that you should apologize for your outburst.**   (The noun clause *that you should apologize for your outburst* is the verb complement.)

**Compound Predicate**   At times a sentence will contain more than one verb, object, or complement. These structures are known as *compound verbs, compound objects,* and *compound complements.*

> The rookie **bats** like Reggie Jackson and **fields** like Willie Mays.   (Two verbs function as the compound verb.)
> I gave the **stove** to Francis and the **bookcase** to Jill.   (The two nouns *stove* and *bookcase* serve as the compound direct object of the verb *gave.*)
> Sammy's week at camp was **long** and **lonely.**   (The two adjectives *long* and *lonely* are the compound complement.)

# Sentence Constructions

English has four basic sentence constructions: simple, compound, complex, and compound-complex sentences. Each construction uses the same basic elements of sentence structure—parts of speech, phrases, and clauses.

## Simple Sentence

The *simple sentence* is an independent clause with no subordinate clauses. It begins with a capital letter and closes with an end mark. Simple sentences can vary considerably in length.

> I bought four apples at the farmers' market.
>
> I bought four apples, a basket of tomatoes, a bag of green beans, and three squashes at the farmers' market.
>
> The farmers' market is a classic example of producers selling directly to consumers and avoiding the attempts of agents to control the supply or to manipulate the price.

## Compound Sentence

The *compound sentence* contains two or more independent clauses but no subordinate clauses. The two independent clauses usually are joined by a comma followed by a conjunction (*and, but, nor, yet*). They may also be joined by a semicolon, a semicolon followed by a linking adverb (*therefore, however, because, since*), or a colon.

> *Conjunction:*      I don't know where he went, **and** no one has seen him since this afternoon.
>
> *Semicolon:*      Harold the First fought in northern Ireland; his campaigns generally were successful.
>
> *Linking adverb:*      Vivian wanted to stay another week in Ashville; **however,** her parents refused to send her more money.
>
> *Colon:*      You must have heard the news: we're all getting bonuses this year!

## Complex Sentence

The *complex sentence* is made up of an independent clause and one or more subordinate clauses. When a subordinate clause introduces the sentence, it is usually followed by a comma unless it is very short. In the following examples, the subordinate clauses are printed in bold type.

> The library closes early in summer **when the students are out of school.**
>
> **After the clear days of Indian summer,** the autumn skies grow heavy and dark.
>
> Linda told us on the phone **that they had had a flat tire last night and that the car wouldn't start this morning.**
>
> **When you come in the front door,** make sure you push it shut, **because the lock doesn't always catch.**

## Compound-Complex Sentence

The *compound-complex sentence* is composed of two or more independent clauses and one or more subordinate clauses. In the examples, the subordinate clauses are printed in bold type.

> John Lennon wrote many ballads, and he recorded them **while he was in England.**
>
> The letter carrier, **who is always punctual,** didn't come today; I wonder if she is ill.
>
> He should telephone you **as soon as he arrives;** but **if for some reason he doesn't call,** tell me immediately.

## Modifiers in Sentences

A *modifier* is any word or group of words which limits or qualifies the meaning of other parts of the sentence. Be sure that your modifiers are clearly joined to the word or words they qualify. Descriptive phrases or clauses joined to the wrong words are known as *dangling modifiers.*

You can correct dangling modifiers by making the doer of the action the subject of the sentence, by adding omitted words, or by changing the phrase to a subordinate clause.

| | |
|---|---|
| *Incorrect:* | Coming over the hill, the blueberries were seen. |
| *Correct:* | Coming over the hill, **we saw** the blueberries in the valley below us. |
| *Incorrect:* | Referring to your request of April 12, the matter is being reviewed by our board. |
| *Correct:* | **Our board is reviewing** your request of April 12 for an additional 122 tons of steel. |
| *Incorrect:* | When she was four years old, her mother died. |
| *Correct:* | **She was four years old when** her mother died. |
| *Incorrect:* | Exhausted and bleary-eyed, the report was finished by the team in the morning. |
| *Correct:* | **The team,** exhausted and bleary-eyed, **finished the report in the morning.** |

# 1.4 Capitalization, Abbreviations, and Numbers

Rules for capitalization, abbreviations, and numbers can be confusing. Not all grammar books agree on the same style. The guidelines in this book are based upon the latest accepted usage.

## Capitalization

Capitalize the first word in any sentence, the personal pronoun *I,* and the first word of a direct quotation if it is a complete statement.

Night falls quickly in the mountains.

The door was open when **I** arrived home.

He looked at the cake and said, "**D**iets, like pie crust, are made to be broken."

### Proper Nouns and Adjectives

Capitalize all proper nouns and adjectives such as the names of persons, business firms, business products, institutions, government bodies and agencies, and public and private organizations.

| | |
|---:|---|
| *Personal names:* | Kareem Abdul-Jabbar, Barbara Walters |
| *Business firm:* | Wal-Mart, Mrs. Field's Cookies |
| *Business products:* | Nissan Sentra, Wisk, Dr. Pepper |
| *Institutions:* | Adler Planetarium, Stanford University |
| *Government bodies and agencies:* | Internal Revenue Service, Civil Rights Commission, Justice Department |
| *Public organizations:* | Junior Chamber of Commerce, Girl Scouts |
| *Private organizations:* | Midwest Authors Guild, JoAnn Kilmer Foundation |

## Hyphenated Names and Prefixes

Capitalize all hyphenated names and hyphenated proper nouns. Also capitalize all proper nouns and adjectives used with a prefix, but do not capitalize the prefix.

Send the bill to Mrs. **Austin-Healy.**

The **Minneapolis-St. Paul** project has been approved.

I am neither **anti-British** nor **pro-French;** I happen to enjoy both countries equally well.

He will always be a **pro-Kennedy** person.

## Family Relationships

Capitalize words describing family relationships only when they substitute for a proper noun or are used with the person's name. Do not capitalize the words if they are used with a possessive pronoun.

I told **Mother** that **my sister** would be late.

She described **her father** to me perfectly.

**Granny Winters** and **Grampa McDonough** are always ready to dance.

We got a letter from **Aunt Helen** and **Uncle Bill.**

Do you know **her cousin Lucia?**

## Nationalities and Races

Capitalize the names of nationalities. Racial groups may be lowercased or capitalized. The only firm rule is *be consistent*. If you capitalize one racial group, capitalize the others as well.

| *Nationalities* | *Racial Groups* |
|---|---|
| Australian | Black *or* black |
| Chinese | White *or* white |
| Indian | |
| Thai | |

## Languages and School Subjects

Capitalize languages and those school subjects followed by a number. Do not capitalize general school subjects unless the subject is a language.

| *Languages* | *School Subjects* |
|---|---|
| Arabic | Biology 403 |
| English | French |
| Korean | history |
| Polish | literature |
| | Social Science 202 |
| | conversational Spanish |
| | statistics |

# Religious Names and Terms

The names of all religions, denominations, and local groups are capitalized.

*Religions*

| | | |
|---|---|---|
| Buddhism | Islam | Shintoism |
| Christianity | Judaism | Taoism |
| Hinduism | | |

*Denominations and Movements*

| | | |
|---|---|---|
| Jehovah's Witnesses | Mormonism | Theosophy |
| Methodism | Sufism | Zen Buddhism |

*Local Groups*

| | |
|---|---|
| Church of the Redeemer | Saint Leonard's House |
| Midwest Baptist Conference | Temple Shalom |

The names of deities and revered persons are capitalized.

| | | |
|---|---|---|
| the Almighty | Child of God | the Word |
| Allah | Jehovah | Logos |
| Lamb of God | Holy Ghost | Mother of God |
| Pan | Shiva | Kwan Yin |
| Kali | Egun-gun | Astarte |

However, pronouns referring to deities are not capitalized in today's style.

---

Capitalize the names of sacred works or highly revered works and their individual parts.

| | | |
|---|---|---|
| the Bible | the Koran | the Book of the Dead |
| the Talmud | the Vedas | the Tripitaka |
| Genesis | the Beatitudes | the Diamond Sutra |
| Apostles' Creed | Epistles | Sermon on the Mount |
| the Decalogue | Book of Job | Acts of the Apostles |

Capitalize religious holidays and terms relating to the eucharistic sacrament.

| | | |
|---|---|---|
| Ascension of the Virgin | High Mass | Passover |
| Christmas | Holy Communion | Ramadan |
| Easter | Lent | Yom Kippur |

Names of other rites and services are not capitalized in a text.

| | | |
|---|---|---|
| baptism | confirmation | seder |
| bar (bas) mitzvah | evening prayer | vesper service |
| confession | matins | worship service |

## Academic Degrees and Personal Titles

Capitalize academic degrees and personal titles used as part of people's names or as a substitute for their names. Titles used after a person's name or by themselves generally are not capitalized.

The exception to the rule occurs when the title refers to the highest national, state, or church office, such as the President of the United States. In such cases, the title may be capitalized.

| | |
|---|---|
| Dr. Marjorie Adamowski | Professor Louise Sasaki |
| Bernard Stone, Ph.D. | Perry Whitehall, M.B.A. |
| President Don Roth | Don Roth, president |
| Director Ellen Tate | Ellen Tate, director |
| Vice-President Quayle | the Vice-President (of U.S.) |
| Cardinal Cody | the Cardinal |
| Pope John Paul II | the Pope |
| Reverend Alice Milano | the reverend |
| General George Custer | the general |
| Admiral Chester Nimitz | the admiral |
| Queen Elizabeth | the Queen |
| Count von Moltke | the count |

## Historic Events, Special Events, and Holidays

Capitalize the names of historic events and periods, special events, holidays, and other publicly recognized special days.

| | |
|---|---|
| Battle of Midway | Midwest Book Fair |
| Black History Month | Mother's Day |
| Columbus Day | National Pickle Week |
| Elizabethan Age | New Year's Day |
| Han Dynasty | Nicene Council |
| Hundred Year War | President's Day |
| Labor Day | Thanksgiving |
| Live AID Africa | World War II |

## Historical Monuments, Places, and Buildings

Capitalize the names of all historical monuments, places, and buildings.

| | |
|---|---|
| Arlington National Cemetery | the Prudential Building |
| the Chicago Loop | Times Square |
| the Latin Quarter | Washington Monument |

# Calendar Days, Months, and Seasons

Capitalize the names of all days of the week and months of the year. Seasons of the year are lowercase unless they are personified.

| | | |
|---|---|---|
| Tuesday | Wednesday | Friday |
| November | June | April |
| fall | winter | summer |

*But:* Have we not seen, Summer, your jeweled nights, your days young and fair?

# Documents

Capitalize the first word and all other words except articles (*a, an, the*) and prepositions under five letters (*in, to, out*) in charters, treaties, declarations, laws, and other official documents. However, when the words *charter, act, treaty,* and *law* are used alone, they generally are not capitalized.

| | |
|---|---|
| Articles of Incorporation | Treaty of Orleans |
| Declaration of Independence | Uniform Commercial Code |
| Magna Carta | Wagner Act |

# Titles of Publications

Capitalize the first word and all other words except articles and prepositions under five letters in the titles of books, chapters, magazines, articles, newspapers, musical compositions, and other publications.

*Girl of the Golden West* (opera)

*No Name in the Streets* (book)

"The Midwest's Blue-collar Blues" (article)

"Do Your Own Tune-ups" (chapter)

*Kansas City Star* (newspaper)

# Compass Points

Points of the compass are not capitalized when they refer simply to direction or are used as adjectives. They are capitalized when they refer to regions of the country.

| | | | |
|---|---|---|---|
| east | north | southwest | eastern |
| west | south | northwest | western |
| the South | the East | the Southwest | the Northeast |
| the North Central states | | | |

# Geographic Names and Regions

Capitalize all geographic names and regions of a country, continent, or hemisphere.

### Cities, Townships, Countries, States, Continents

| | | |
|---|---|---|
| California | New York | South America |
| India | Niles Township | Western Hemisphere |

### Islands, Peninsulas, Straits, Beaches

| | | |
|---|---|---|
| Baja Peninsula | Strait of Magellan | Myrtle Beach |
| Canary Islands | Strait of Malacca | Seal Island |

### Bodies of Water

| | | |
|---|---|---|
| Aegean Sea | Nile River | Victoria Falls |
| Lake Tahoe | Tinker Creek | Walden Pond |

### Mountains and Mountain Chains

| | | |
|---|---|---|
| the Andes | Kilimanjaro | Mount Fuji |
| Cascade Mountains | Mount Everest | Pike's Peak |

### Parks, Forests, Canyons, Dams

| | |
|---|---|
| Aswan Dam | Humboldt Redwoods Forest |
| Bright Angel Canyon | Serengeti National Preserve |
| Hoover Dam | Yosemite National Park |

# Scientific Terms

The rules for capitalizing scientific terms, particularly the divisions of plants and animals, can be complex and bewildering. This section presents some general rules for capitalizing the more common terms that are likely to be used.

**Common Names of Plants and Animals**    Usually, lowercase the names of plants and animals, capitalizing only proper nouns and adjectives used with the names. Check with a dictionary to be sure of accuracy.

| | |
|---|---|
| black-eyed Susan | rhesus monkey |
| Cooper's hawk | Rhode Island red |
| border collie | Rocky Mountain sheep |
| golden retriever | rose of Sharon |
| jack-in-the pulpit | Thomson's gazelle |
| mustang | thoroughbred |
| Persian cat | white leghorn fowl |

**Geological Terms**    Capitalize the names of eras, periods, epochs, and episodes but not the words *era, period,* and so on used with the term.

| | |
|---|---|
| Ice Age (reference to Pleistocene glacial epoch) | |
| Lower Jurassic period | Pliocene epoch |
| Paleozoic era | Precambrian period |

**Astronomical Terms**  Capitalize all proper names of asteroids, planets and their satellites, constellations, and other astronomical phenomena. In many cases, *earth, sun,* and *moon* are lowercased unless used with other planets in a sentence.

| | | |
|---|---|---|
| Alpha Centuri | the Crab nebula | Milky Way |
| Andromeda Galaxy | Demos | North Star |
| Arcturus | Halley's Comet | Orion |
| Big Dipper | the Leonids | Pleiades |
| Cassiopeia | Mercury | Saturn |

Descriptive terms that apply to unique astronomical or meteorological phenomena are not capitalized.

| | |
|---|---|
| aurora borealis | meteor shower |
| blizzard | sun dogs |
| hurricane | tornado |
| the rings of Jupiter | the moons of Uranus |

**Medical Terms**  Lowercase the names of diseases, syndromes, symptoms, tests, drugs, and the like. Capitalize only proper nouns and adjectives or trade names used with these terms.

| | |
|---|---|
| aspirin | Parkinson's disease |
| finger-nose test | poliomyelitis |
| Guillain-Barré syndrome | Salk vaccine |
| infectious granuloma | tetracycline |
| Metymid | Tylenol |

**Physical and Chemical Terms**  Lowercase laws, theorems, principles, and the like, capitalizing only proper nouns and adjectives used with these terms. Chemical symbols are also capitalized and set without periods.

| | |
|---|---|
| Boyle's law | Maxwell's equations |
| $C^{14}$ or C-14 | Newton's second law |
| carbon 14 | Planck's constant |
| general theory of relativity | sulfuric acid |
| $H_2SO_4$ | $U^{238}$ or U-238 |
| Lorenz transformations | uranium 238 |

## Capitals with Numbers

Capitalize a noun or abbreviation before a number when it designates a formal part of a written work.

| | |
|---|---|
| Act V, Scene 3 | Paragraph 3 or Para. 3 |
| Book IV | Section 44 or Sec. 44 |
| Chapter 14 or Chap. 14 | Unit 3 |

# Abbreviations

The style for abbreviations has gone through a series of changes in the past few decades. The trend today is to drop the periods from most abbreviations. However, in this book we retain the traditional periods to show which abbreviations have omitted them in the past.

Periods may be omitted if the writer is consistent. If *AM* appears without periods in one sentence, do not use *A.M.* in another.

## General Guidelines

Here are some general guidelines for using abbreviations.

**1. In abbreviations with internal periods (Ph.D., B.C., N.W.), there should be no space after the first period.**

**2. Initials of personal names, however, are followed by regular spacing (H. G. Wells).**

**3. When in doubt about how to style abbreviations of personal or company names, always check with the individual or firm to see how they prefer the abbreviation to be written.**

## Personal Names and Titles

**Personal Names**    Avoid using abbreviations for given names except when transcribing a signature.

Dorothy Brandt *not* Dor. Brandt
Charles Villiard *not* Chas. Villiard

If the signature is written with abbreviations, follow the style of the author.

Yours truly,                          Sincerely yours,
Geo. C. Kelly                       L. K. Geng

Some publications and business writers omit the periods following initials. However, for convenience and clarity it is usually good practice to use periods with all initials given with names.

Caroline S. Wilson               Robert J. Edwards
B. G. Honicutt                      A. Teresa Valdez

If the person is referred to by initials only, no periods are used.

FDR (Franklin Delano Roosevelt)
LBJ (Lyndon Baines Johnson)
HD (Hilda Dolittle)

**Titles Before Names**   Social titles are always abbreviated whether used with the surname only or the full name. Notice which titles are used with or without periods.

| | |
|---|---|
| Mrs. Gloria Greenberg | Mr. Valentine Cancilleri |
| Ms. Barbara Walnum | M. Tricia (Thomas) Benton |
| Mme Cecilia Payne | Mlle Jane Tild |
| Messrs. Paul Mori and Norman Zuefle | Dr. Evelyn Veach |

When a civil or military title is used with the surname alone, it is spelled out. When the full name is used, the title is abbreviated.

| | |
|---|---|
| General Sherman | Senator Collins |
| Committeeman Shapiro | Mayor Daley |
| Congresswoman Rush | Captain Kirk |
| | |
| Lt. Col. Ruth Claire | Capt. James T. Kirk |
| Sen. Paul Simon | Hon. Carmen Gilead |
| Ald. Yvonne Carlos | Gov. Peter Tsing |

Titles *Reverend* and *Honorable* are spelled out if they are preceded by *the*. They may also be used with social titles. *Reverend* is never used with the surname alone, but the title may be abbreviated when used with the person's full name.

| | |
|---|---|
| the Reverend Betty J. Dell | the Rev. Betty J. Dell |
| the Right Reverend Monsignor Carl L. Bernard | the Rt. Rev. Msr. Carl L. Bernard |
| the Honorable Wilson O. Justman | the Hon. Wilson O. Justman |

**Titles After Names**   Titles, degrees, affiliations, or the designation *Jr.* (junior), *Sr.* (senior), *II, III* (or 2d, 3d) following a person's name are considered part of that name. While the abbreviations *Jr.* and *Sr.* are set off from the name by commas, the designations *II, III, 2d,* or *3d* are not set off by commas. These abbreviations are used only with the full name, never just the surname (*Mrs. Gregory Young, Jr.*, not *Mrs. Young, Jr.*).

| | |
|---|---|
| Njoki Salumbe, Ph.D. | Richard Butzen, LL.D. |
| Daniel Cronon III, M.A. | Whitney Rune, Sr. |

The abbreviation *Esq.* (*Esquire*) refers to someone who is a lawyer and is never used when another title is given, whether before or after the name.

Sue Allen, Esq.   *not*   Ms. Sue Allen, Esq.

Carl Hanson, Esq.   *not*   Carl Hanson, Esq., Ph.D.

Social titles are also dropped if another title is used following the name.

Harriet Long, M.F.A.   *not*   Miss Harriet Long, M.F.A.

**Names with *Saint***   When *saint* precedes the person's name, it is often abbreviated *St.*, although many prefer to spell the word out.

**St.** Catherine de Sienna   *or*   **Saint** Catherine de Sienna

*Saint* is generally omitted before the names of apostles, evangelists, and church founders.

Matthew, John, Luke, Mark

Paul, John the Baptist

Augustine, Jerome

When *saint* is used as part of a personal name, follow the style preferred by the individual.

Ruth St. Denis

Adele St. Claire Hutchins

Alfred George Saint-Augustine

## Company Names

The following abbreviations are commonly used as part of firm names.

| | |
|---|---|
| & (and) | Inc. (incorporated) |
| Assoc. (association, associates, associated) | Ltd. (limited) |
| Bro., Bros. (brothers) | Mfg. (manufacturing) |
| Co. (company) | RR, Ry (railroad) |
| Corp. (corporation) | |

Abbreviations of company names may or may not use periods. Make sure you determine how the company itself prefers to spell its name. Some of the more common abbreviations include the following:

| | |
|---|---|
| IBM | Gor-Tex, Inc. |
| Ford Motor Co. | AT&T |
| Wm. C. Brown Publishers, Ltd. | MCI |

## Agencies and Organizations

The names of government agencies, network broadcasting companies, associations, fraternal and service organizations, unions, and other groups are usually abbreviated without periods. However, some publications such as *The New York Times* will print them with periods. Whichever style is used, it is important to be consistent.

*Unions*

AFL-CIO (American Federation of Labor—Congress of Industrial Organizations)

UMW (United Mine Workers)

UAW (United Auto Workers)

*Government Agencies*

HHS (Department of Health and Human Services)
DOT (Department of Transportation)
CIA (Central Intelligence Agency)

*Social Organizations*

BSA (Boy Scouts of America)
YWCA (Young Women's Christian Association)
DAR (Daughters of the American Revolution)
VFW (Veterans of Foreign Wars)

*Professional Organizations*

PEN (Poets, Editors, and Novelists)
AMA (American Medical Association)

## Geographic Terms

**Address and State Abbreviations**  Address abbreviations may be used with or without periods and may be set in all capitals or in initial capitals only. The U.S. Postal Service recommends using all capitals without periods for address abbreviations. Following is a list of the most common abbreviations used in addresses.

| | | | |
|---|---|---|---|
| Avenue | AVE, Ave. | Point | PT, Pt. |
| Expressway | EXPY, Expy. | Ridge | RDG, Rdg. |
| Hospital | HOSP, Hosp. | River | RV, Rv. |
| Heights | HTS, Hts. | Road | RD, Rd. |
| Institute | INST, Inst. | Rural | R, R. |
| Junction | JCT, Jct. | Shore | SH, Sh. |
| Lake | LK, Lk. | Square | SQ, Sq. |
| Lakes | LKS, Lks. | Station | STA, Sta. |
| Lane | LN, Ln. | Terrace | TER, Ter. |
| Meadows | MDWS, Mdws. | Turnpike | TPKE, Tpke. |
| Mountain | MT, Mt. | Union | UN, Un. |
| Palms | PLMS, Plms. | View | VW, Vw. |
| Park | PK, Pk. | Village | VLG, Vlg. |
| Parkway | PKY, Pky. | | |

Points of the compass following a street name are used without periods. If they precede the name, periods are used.

147 Eastwood NW                   1737 Fifth Street SE
6 N. Michigan                     2320 E. Grand

Use the postal Zip Code abbreviations for states, territories, and Canadian provinces. The abbreviations are capitalized and contain no punctuation.

*State Abbreviations*

| | |
|---|---|
| Alabama   AL | Nebraska   NE |
| Alaska   AK | Nevada   NV |
| Arizona   AZ | New Hampshire   NH |
| Arkansas   AR | New Jersey   NJ |
| California   CA | New Mexico   NM |
| Colorado   CO | New York   NY |
| Connecticut   CT | North Carolina   NC |
| Delaware   DE | North Dakota   ND |
| Florida   FL | Ohio   OH |
| Georgia   GA | Oklahoma   OK |
| Hawaii   HI | Oregon   OR |
| Idaho   ID | Pennsylvania   PA |
| Illinois   IL | Rhode Island   RI |
| Indiana   IN | South Carolina   SC |
| Iowa   IA | South Dakota   SD |
| Kansas   KS | Tennessee   TN |
| Kentucky   KY | Texas   TX |
| Louisiana   LA | Utah   UT |
| Maine   ME | Vermont   VT |
| Maryland   MD | Virginia   VA |
| Massachusetts   MA | Washington   WA |
| Michigan   MI | West Virginia   WV |
| Minnesota   MN | Wisconsin   WI |
| Mississippi   MS | Wyoming   WY |
| Missouri   MO | District of Columbia   DC |
| Montana   MT | |

*Foreign Abbreviations*

| | |
|---|---|
| Canal Zone   CZ | Guam   GU |
| Puerto Rico   PR | Virgin Islands   VI |
| Alberta   AB | British Columbia   BC |
| Manitoba   MB | New Brunswick   NB |
| Newfoundland   NF | Northwest Territories   NT |
| Nova Scotia   NS | Ontario   ON |
| Prince Edward Island   PE | Quebec   PQ |
| Saskatchewan   SK | Yukon Territory   YT |
| Labrador   LB | |

**Names of Countries**   The names of countries should be spelled out whenever possible. When abbreviated, however, periods should be used after each part of the name. There is generally no space after the first period.

| | |
|---|---|
| England | Engl. |
| France | Fr. |
| Germany | Ger. |
| Italy | It. |
| Russia | Rus. |
| Spain | Sp. |
| Sweden | Swe. |
| United Kingdom | U.K. or G.B. (Great Britain) |
| United States | U.S. |

For the correct abbreviations for other countries, consult a good dictionary or world atlas.

**Place Names**   Prefixes such as *fort, mount, point,* and the like used with geographic names should not be abbreviated unless space must be saved in the text.

| | |
|---|---|
| Fort Wayne | Ft. Wayne |
| Mount Everest | Mt. Everest |
| Point Townsend | Pt. Townsend |
| South Orange | S. Orange |

Many grammarians make an exception of names beginning with *saint* and abbreviate the prefix in all cases. However, the prefixes *san* and *santa* are not abbreviated.

| | |
|---|---|
| San Cristobal | St. Lawrence Seaway |
| Santa Barbara | St. Louis |

**Points of the Compass**   The following symbols are used to abbreviate points of the compass.

| | |
|---|---|
| N, S, E, W | NE, SE, NW, SW |
| S by SE | N by NW |

*Latitude* and *longitude* are never abbreviated when used alone. In technical notation, the terms are abbreviated and the compass symbols inserted following the degrees of latitude and longitude.

twenty-two degrees south latitude

longitude 54° 57′west

lat. 42° 57′.3 N

long. 90° 27′.5 W

# Time

**Time of Day**    Abbreviations that indicate time of day or night may be set in all capitals or lowercase. Most grammar books agree that periods are used in either case.

| | | |
|---|---|---|
| A.M., a.m. | (ante meridiem) | before noon |
| M. | (meridian) | noon |
| P.M., p.m. | (post meridiem) | after noon |

**Days of the Week, Months of the Year**    The names of the days of the week can be abbreviated in the following way:

Monday   Mon.
Tuesday   Tues.
Wednesday   Wed.
Thursday   Thurs.
Friday   Fri.
Saturday   Sat.
Sunday   Sun.

Months of the year are abbreviated as follows:

January   Jan.
February   Feb.
March   Mar.
April   Apr.
May   May
June   June
July   July
August   Aug.
September   Sept.
October   Oct.
November   Nov.
December   Dec.

**Years**    Accepted abbreviations mark the years before and after the birth of Christ.

A.D. (*anno Domini*—means in the year of the Lord) This abbreviation precedes the year.

William the Conqueror landed on British shores in **A.D. 1066.**

B.C. (*before Christ*) This abbreviation follows the year.

Alexander the Great died in the summer of **323 B.C.**

## Scholarly Abbreviations

The rules for use of abbreviations in scholarship are widely agreed upon and include the following:

**1. Abbreviations should be kept out of the body of the text as much as possible, except in technical matters.**

**2. Abbreviations such as *e.g.*, *i.e.*, and *etc.* should be used primarily in parenthetical material.**

**3. Scholarly abbreviations such as *ibid.*, *cf.*, *s.v.* and *op.cit.* should be used only in footnotes, bibliographical material, and general notes to the text.**

Following is a partial list of some of the more familiar scholarly abbreviations. For a complete list, consult a dictionary, scholarly handbook, or more detailed grammar text.

| | |
|---|---|
| anon. | anonymous |
| biog. | biography |
| cf. | *confer*, compare |
| cont. | continued |
| def. | definition, definite |
| div. | division |
| e.g. | *exempli gratia*, for example |
| esp. | especially |
| hdqrs. | headquarters |
| i.e. | *id est*, that is |
| lit. | literally |
| mgr. | manager |
| n.a. | not applicable, not available |
| pp. | pages |
| rev. | review, revised, revision |
| subj. | subject |
| trans. | translation, translated |
| vol. | volume |
| yr. | your, year |

## Measures

Abbreviations for units of measure are the same whether the unit is singular or plural.

**English Measure** The abbreviations for length, area, and volume are as follows:

| *Length* | | *Area* | | *Volume* | |
|---|---|---|---|---|---|
| in. | inch | sq. in. | square inch | cu. in. | cubic inch |
| ft. | foot, feet | sq. ft. | square foot | cu. ft. | cubic foot |
| yd. | yard | sq. yd. | square yard | cu. yd. | cubic yard |
| rd. | rod | sq. rd. | square rod | | |
| mi. | mile | sq. mi. | square mile | | |
| | | a. | acre | | |

Abbreviations for weight and capacity reflect the complicated English system of measures. There are three systems in use: *avoirdupois* the common system; *troy* used by jewelers; and *apothecaries'* measure. Although the metric system is being adopted in this country, these other systems are still in use. The abbreviations are as follows:

| *Weight* | | *Dry Measure* | | *Liquid Measure* | |
|---|---|---|---|---|---|
| gr. | grain | pt. | pint | min. | minim |
| s. | scruple | qt. | quart | fl. dr. | fluid dram |
| dr. | dram | pk. | peck | fl. oz. | fluid ounce |
| dwt. | pennyweight | bu. | bushel | gi. | gill |
| oz. | ounce | c. | cup | pt. | pint |
| lb. | pound | tsp. | teaspoon | qt. | quart |
| cwt. | hundredweight | tbl. | tablespoon | gal. | gallon |
| tn. | ton | | | bbl. | barrel |

English abbreviations for the standard units of time are as follows:

| sec. | second | h., hr. | hour |
|---|---|---|---|
| min. | minute | d. | day |
| mo. | month | yr. | year |

**Metric System**   The metric system, long used in scientific publications, is gradually becoming the national system of weights and measures. The basic units of measure are the liter, gram, and meter. The following abbreviations are used with metric measurements:

| *Length* | | *Area* | | *Volume* | |
|---|---|---|---|---|---|
| mm | millimeter | sq. mm | square millimeter | $mm^3$ | cubic millimeter |
| cm | centimeter | sq. cm | square centimeter | cc | cubic centimeter |
| dm | decimeter | sq. dm | square decimeter | $dm^3$ | cubic decimeter |
| m | meter | sq. m | square meter | $m^3$ | cubic meter |
| dam | dekameter | sq. dam | square dekameter | | |
| ca | centare | sq. ca | square centare | | |
| ha | hectare | sq. ha | square hectare | | |
| km | kilometer | sq. km | square kilometer | | |

| *Capacity* | | *Weight* | |
|---|---|---|---|
| ml | milliter | mg | milligram |
| cl | centiliter | cg | centigram |
| dl | deciliter | dg | decagram |
| l | liter | g | gram |
| dal | dekaliter | dag | dekagram |
| hl | hectoliter | hg | hectogram |
| kl | kiloliter | kg | kilogram |

## Science and Technology

The International System of Units (SI) is generally used by scientists around the world to label measurements. SI is roughly equivalent to the metric system. In some cases, however, the method of forming abbreviations differs among the various disciplines of science. For a full listing of scientific abbreviations, consult a technical handbook or scientific style book.

Following are the seven fundamental SI units, termed base units, that serve as the foundation terms in science.

| *Term* | *Unit* | *Abbreviation* |
|---|---|---|
| length | meter | m |
| mass | kilogram | kg |
| time | second | s |
| electric current | ampere | A |
| thermodynamic temp. | kelvin | K |
| amount of substance | mole | mol |
| luminous intensity | candela | cd |

The abbreviations used by various branches of science may or may not be related to the International System. Following is a partial list of the more commonly used abbreviations. Notice that they are set without periods.

| | | | |
|---|---|---|---|
| AC | alternating current | AM | amplitude modulation |
| AU | astronomic unit | BP | boiling point |
| cal | calorie | CP | candle power |
| CPS | cycles per second | DC | direct current |
| FM | frequency modulation | HP | horsepower |
| kw | kilowatt | MPG | miles per gallon |
| MPH | miles per hour | neg | negative |
| pH | acidity or alkalinity | RPM | revolutions per minute |
| std | standard | temp | temperature |
| UT or UTC | universal time | | |

## Commercial Abbreviations

Abbreviations used in business and commerce follow a varied style. The most commonly used abbreviations and their accepted styles are given here.

| | | | |
|---|---|---|---|
| acct. | account | agt. | agent |
| a/v | ad valorem | bal. | balance |
| bbl. | barrel | bdl. | bundle |
| bu. | bushel | c.l. | carload |
| COD | cash on delivery | cr. | credit, creditor |
| cwt. | hundredweight | doz. | dozen |
| dr. | debit, debitor | ea. | each |
| f.o.b. | free on board | gro. | gross |

# Numbers

As in the case with capitalization and abbreviations, the rules for handling numbers in text are complex and varied. In this book, we provide guidelines that are generally agreed upon by many experts.

## Arabic and Roman Numerals

Most of the figures used today are expressed in Arabic numbers. However, Roman numerals are still used in names, documents, books, dates, and so on. Following is a list of Arabic numbers and their equivalents in Roman numerals.

| Arabic | Roman | Arabic | Roman | Arabic | Roman |
|--------|-------|--------|--------|--------|-------|
| 1 | I | 16 | XVI | 90 | XC |
| 2 | II | 17 | XVII | 100 | C |
| 3 | III | 18 | XVIII | 200 | CC |
| 4 | IV | 19 | XIX | 300 | CCC |
| 5 | V | 20 | XX | 400 | CD |
| 6 | VI | 21 | XXI | 500 | D |
| 7 | VII | 22 | XXII | 600 | DC |
| 8 | VIII | 23 | XXIII | 700 | DCC |
| 9 | IX | 24 | XXIV | 800 | DCCC |
| 10 | X | 25 | XXV | 900 | CM |
| 11 | XI | 26 | XXVI | 1000 | M |
| 12 | XII | 27 | XXVII | 2000 | MM |
| 13 | XIII | 28 | XXVIII | 3000 | MMM |
| 14 | XIV | 29 | XXIX | 4000 | $M\bar{V}$ |
| 15 | XV | 30 | XXX | 5000 | $\bar{V}$ |

## Figures or Words

Whether numbers should be spelled out or written in figures depends on several factors. Among them are the size of the figure, what it stands for, and what kind of text it appears in—business, personal, scientific, or scholarly.

In general, use the "rule of ten" in determining whether to spell out a number or express it in figures. Under the rule of ten, spell out numbers ten and under (two, five, seven) and any number that is divisible by ten (twenty, sixty, eighty). All other numbers over ten are written in figures.

Governors from **six** western states urged passage of the water rights bill.

I ordered **three** dozen boxes of mint candies.

Did you know this book has **1,345** pages?

She turned **39** last year but doesn't look over **25.**

Our flight will arrive in Hong Kong in **12** hours.

We now have a **thirty**-year mortgage to pay off.

**Round Numbers** Numbers used as approximations in place of specific figures are often spelled out, even when expressed as hundreds of thousands.

The concert drew an estimated **thirty thousand** fans.

About **three hundred thousand** people were left homeless by the floods.

Some form of sun worship has existed for nearly **ten thousand** years in human history.

Very large numbers are usually expressed in figures followed by *million, billion, trillion,* and so on.

It would cost **$3.5 trillion** to send a piloted probe to Jupiter.

The gross national product is nearly **$257 billion.**

The greater metropolitan Chicago area contains over **7.2 million** people.

**Ordinal Numbers** The same rule of ten holds for ordinal numbers (*first, second, third*) as well.

Janet ranked **fifth** in a class of 356 students.

My two horses came in **first** and **ninth** in the afternoon race.

The **25th** article in the bylaws hasn't been revised.

Bjorn was given the **232d** and **233d** numbers out of 655.

Notice that the form for *second* and *third* is *d* and not *nd* or *rd*.

**Consistency** The exception to the rule of ten occurs when numbers under and over ten are used in the same paragraph, in a series, or to refer to the same item in a sentence. For the sake of consistency, numbers under ten are frequently expressed in figures.

Joan's family has **5** children, **11** cats, **3** turtles, **15** gerbils, and **2** canaries.

In **ten** years, the population has grown from about **8,000** to **154,567.** (*Ten* is spelled out because it is not related to the population figures but stands by itself. Compare that sentence to *In the past 10–15 years, the population has grown from about 8,000 to 154,567.*)

We climbed the **102**–story building all the way to the top, but **four** of us had trouble making the last **2 or 3** stories. (The figures *2* and *3* refer to the same item—the number of stories. *Four,* however, refers to a separate category, the number of people, and is therefore spelled out.)

**Numbers Together** In some instances, numbers are used for more than one item in a sentence. Generally, the smaller of the two figures will be expressed in words.

We developed **twenty-five 35 mm** slides yesterday.

The stock cars will go **14 two-mile** laps.

I'd like **250 thirty-cent** stamps.

He bought **twelve 65-cent** labels.

**First Word in a Sentence**    Spell out numbers that begin a sentence, regardless of any inconsistency this may create in the rest of the sentence or paragraph. As a general rule, if the sentence contains more than one figure, or if the figure is large, try to rephrase the sentence so that the number does not come first.

**Twenty-seven** people attended the banquet.

**Fifteen** cars piled up on the freeway, and **37** cars blocked the exit ramp.

> *Avoid:*    **Twenty** out of every **100** people interviewed preferred daytime baseball games.
>
> *Better:*    Daytime baseball games were preferred by **20** out of every **100** people interviewed.
> *or*
> We found that **20** out of every **100** people interviewed preferred daytime baseball games.
>
> *Avoid:*    **Nineteen twenty-seven** marked the first solo transatlantic flight in aviation history.
>
> *Better:*    The year **1927** marked the first solo transatlantic flight in aviation history.

## Ages

Express exact ages in figures. Approximate ages can be expressed in words or figures but be sure to use the same style throughout.

Theodore Roosevelt was elected Vice President when he was only **42.**

Andria is **7** and Van is **14.**

The baby is **2** years and **6** months old.

She was about **60** when she first traveled to Africa.

My father is nearly **ninety.**

## Names

Roman numerals are used to distinguish among male members of the same family who have identical names. No comma is used between the name and Roman numerals.

John Ellis **III**                                    Bror von Blixen **IV**

Roman numerals are also used to differentiate sovereigns, emperors, and popes with the same name. Modern usage, however, permits Arabic numerals in some cases.

John **XXIII**    *or*    John **23d**
Elizabeth **II**          Richard **III**

Vehicles such as ships, spacecraft, cars, and airplanes may also be given Roman numerals to distinguish them from previous models with the same name. Although earlier spacecraft in the NASA program carried Roman numerals, current practice is to use Arabic numbers.

| | |
|---|---|
| *America **IV*** | *Bluebird **III*** |
| *Mercury **II*** | *Apollo **12*** |
| *Bell X-15* | *Saturn **2*** |

## Governmental Designations

**Governments**   Ordinal numbers are used to designate particular dynasties, governments, and governing bodies in a succession. The numbers are spelled out if they are less than one hundred and precede the noun. In most cases, they are capitalized.

| | |
|---|---|
| the **102d** Congress | **Third** Reich |
| **First** Continental Congress | **Twelfth** Dynasty |
| **Eighty-sixth** Congress | **Fourth** Republic |

**Political Divisions**   Numbers one hundred or less indicating political divisions should be spelled out in ordinal form and capitalized.

| | |
|---|---|
| **Forty-second** Ward | **Thirty-fifth** Precinct |
| **123d** Congressional District | Circuit Court of Appeals for the **Sixth** Court |

**Military Units**   Spell out in ordinal form numbers one hundred or less that indicate military subdivisions.

| | |
|---|---|
| the **101st** Airborne | **Eighty-sixth** Regiment |
| **156th** Fighter Wing | **Seventh** Fleet |
| Second Batallion, **110th** Artillery | |

## Organizations

**Unions and Lodges**   Use Arabic numbers to express figures designating local branches of labor unions and of fraternal lodges.

Masonic Lodge No. **335**

Flight Attendants Union Local No. **127**

American Legion Post No. **34**

**Churches**   Spell out ordinal numbers used with religious organizations or houses of worship.

> **First** United Methodist Church
> **Seventh**-day Adventists
> **Twenty-second** Church of Christ, Scientist
> **Second** Baptist Church

**Corporations and Civic Events**   Numbers used in the names of companies or civic events may be spelled out or expressed in figures or Roman numerals. You will need to follow the particular organization's style.

> **First** National Bank              **1st** Federal Savings & Loan
> **3rd** Annual Sport Jamboree        **XXIV** Olympics

## Addresses and Thoroughfares

House numbers should be expressed in figures, except for the number *one*. Numbered streets *one* through *ten* are spelled out.

> **One** East Superior                **354** Crain Street
> 1274 - **23d** Street                 32 **Second** Avenue

When the address is part of a building's name, the number is usually spelled out.

> **One** Magnificent Mile
> **Thirty-Three** Park Ridge

Use figures for all state, interstate, and federal highways.

> U.S. Route **66** (U.S. 66)
> Interstate **294** (I-294)
> Arizona **103**
> County Line **24**

## Time of Day

When time is expressed in even, half, or quarter hours, the numbers are generally spelled out.

> The movie starts at a **quarter past four.**
> I didn't get home until **midnight** last night.
> The meeting is set for **two o'clock** this Thursday.

Figures are used when the exact time is given or in designations of time with *A.M.* or *P.M.* Never use *o'clock* in either of these cases.

The train pulled into Lisbon at **12:33** in the morning.

The full report should be on the **6:30** news.

Precisely at **5:00,** I saw him leave his apartment.

We'll meet here again at **5:15 P.M.** tomorrow.

He called at **12:20 A.M.** to say he had locked himself out of his house.

In the 24-hour time system, figures are always used. There is no punctuation between the hour and minutes.

Our ship docks at **0615** on Wednesday.

Registration hours are from **0900** to **1130** and **1300** to **1530** every day except Sunday.

## Dates

**Day and Month**    When writing dates, use the current style (either day/month/ year or month/day/year).

On **7 August 1975,** we left for Egypt.

I sent the letter on **April 14, 1983,** but I never received a reply.

Notice that when the month/day/year form is used, the year is set off by commas before and after it.

When the day and month are used alone, references to another date in the same month are spelled out.

The order was dated **6 July.** We sent your package out on the **seventh.**

You may use either words or figures for the day when it occurs alone or when the month is part of a prepositional phrase in a sentence.

Paychecks are issued on the **5th** of each month.
Paychecks are issued on the **fifth** of each month.

On the **12th of April,** I signed the contract.
On the **twelfth of April,** I signed the contract.

**Month and Year**    When dates are identified only by month and year, no internal punctuation is necessary.

She entered school in **September 1979** when she turned 21.

**The Year Alone or Abbreviated**    Years are expressed in numbers no matter how large or small they may be. No commas are used in the figure.

The Egyptian Nile Valley was heavily populated by **3500 B.C.**

Early records indicate the settlement was occupied from **34 B.C.** to **A.D. 67.**

Abbreviations of years drop the first two figures and substitute an apostrophe.

the class of **'69**                                    the spirit of **'76**

They were married in **'41.**

**Centuries and Decades**    References to particular centuries and decades are spelled out in lowercase letters.

We are nearing the end of the **twentieth century.**

Social upheaval during the **sixties** gave way to political conservatism in the **eighties.**

If decades are identified by century, be sure to use the same style throughout.

> *Incorrect:*    The **1880s** and **'90s** were a time of colonial expansion.
> *Correct:*    The **1880s** and **1890s** were a time of colonial expansion.

Notice that there is no apostrophe before the final *s* after the year.

**Ears**    Use figures to express dates and words to express centuries whether the era designation comes before or after the date involved. The most frequently used era designations are as follows:

B.C.    before Christ (twelfth century B.C.)

A.D.    (*anno Domini*) in the year of the Lord (A.D. 1940)

A.H.    (*anno Hegirae*) in the year of (Muhammad's) Hegira

A.H.    (*anno Hebraico*) in the Hebrew year

B.P.    before the present

The designations A.D. and A.H. precede the figures, while the other designations follow them. However, both A.D. and B.C. follow centuries expressed in words.

378 B.C.                                    A.D. 1945

13,400 B.P.                                    A.H. 677

fourth century B.C.                                    fifteenth century A.D.

## Money

Use figures to express sums of money whether foreign or U.S. currency. However, spell out small sums of money when the figure stands alone or serves as an adjective.

> The car cost **$2560.**
>
> I changed **$4** for **£6.**
>
> I remember when movies cost **twenty-five cents.**
>
> They charge a **ten-cent** fee.

If an abbreviation rather than a symbol is used for foreign currency, leave a space between the abbreviation and the figure.

> Fr 456   (French francs)
>
> DM 145   (German deutsche marks)

When two currencies share the same symbol (for example, the $ symbol in Canadian and U.S. money), use a prefix or suffix to distinguish between the two.

> His hotel bill totaled **$127.50 Canadian ($87.50 U.S.)** for a three-day stay.

**Fractional and Large Amounts**   Fractional amounts over one dollar are expressed in figures. Very large amounts may be expressed in figures and units of million, billion, or trillion.

> I bought this book for **$12.00** and then saw the same item on sale for **$3.50.**
>
> The clerk added up the charges of **$66.21, $43.90,** and **$23.10.**
>
> A painting valued at **$3.2 million** was stolen from the galley.

Notice that when whole numbers and fractional amounts are used together, ciphers are used after the whole number *($12.00, $3.50).*

## Percentages

In general, percentages are expressed in figures followed by the word *percent.* In scientific and statistical material, the symbol % is used.

> Glenn's NOW account earns **7 percent** interest.
>
> There is a **50 percent** chance of snow tomorrow.
>
> Only **25%** of the blood samples tested yielded positive results.
>
> Power outage rose by **15%** when the additional current was used.

## Fractions and Decimals

Mixed fractions and decimals are expressed in figures. For clarity, decimal fractions of less than 1.00 may be preceded by a zero.

**24½** feet by **34¼** feet
up to **2.25** centimeters
a ratio of **0.56** (or .56)
the CPI rose **1.5** percent

If several decimal fractions are used in a sentence or paragraph, make sure they have the same number of places to the right of the decimal point.

| | |
|---|---|
| *Incorrect:* | The variable rates for January were **.75** percent, **.4** percent, and **.96** percent. |
| *Correct:* | The variable rates for January were **.75** percent, **.40** percent, and **.96** percent. |

Simple fractions are expressed in words. If the fraction is used as an adjective, it is hyphenated. If it serves as a noun, it is two words.

**one-fifth** share of the market
**two-thirds** majority

**one tenth** of their income
**one quarter** of the workers

## Measures

In scientific and many business texts, physical quantities such as distances, lengths, areas, volumes, pressures, weights, and the like are expressed in figures whether they are whole numbers or fractions.

| | |
|---|---|
| **125** miles | **87** meters |
| **450** volts | **4** pounds **10** ounces |
| **.32** centimeter | **10°** of arc |
| **98.6°** Fahrenheit | **60** acres |

In ordinary text matter, fractions may be written out. However, where fractions and whole numbers appear together, use figures to express both numbers.

The airport is about **three quarters** of a mile from here.

Give me a sheet of paper **8½** by **11** inches.

She ordered another box of **3½-by-5½**-inch cards.

If abbreviations or symbols are used for the unit of measure, the quantity should be expressed in figures.

| | | |
|---|---|---|
| 3¾ mi. | 6 V | 35 mm film |
| 25 MPH | 32 g | 30 cc |
| 5″ by 7″ | 10%-15% | 36° 30′N |

## Temperature

Temperature is expressed in figures with the degree sign plus the scale being used.

15° F (Fahrenheit)                                   − 20° C (Celsius or centigrade)
12° K (Kelvin)

## Parts of a Book

Generally, major book divisions are expressed in Roman numerals and minor divisions in Arabic figures. However, follow the style used in each book.

The material in **Part I, chapters 6–12** covers how to re-upholster your couch.

Plates, figures, tables, pages, and so on are also set in Arabic figures. The only general exception to this rule occurs in the preliminary or introductory pages of a book, which are usually set in Roman numerals.

Be sure to read pages **i–ix** before starting Chapter 1.

Plate **7** in Chapter 23 provides an excellent illustration of a ring-tailed duck.

I don't think figure **3.1** is accurate.

He has the final numbers for tables **2–4.**

## Inclusive Numbers

Use the following guidelines for inclusive numbers.

1. **For numbers less than 100, use all digits.**
   4–23      86–92
2. **For 100 or multiples of 100, use all digits.**
   100–104   500–563
3. **For 101 through 109 (and multiples of 100), use only the changed digits.**
   101–4      503–6      1006–9
4. **For 110 through 199 (and multiples of 100), use two digits or more as needed.**
   112–24    467–68    1389–91   14285–389

Continued numbers other than pages are written in the following style:

the winter of **1980–1981**                the years **1234–1345**
fiscal year **1984–85**                       A.D. **712–14**
**243–221** B.C. (all digits are used with B.C. years)

When an inclusive date is used in a title, all digits are usually repeated.

*Brian Gregory's Journals: 1745–1789*
World War II: **1939–1945**

# 1.5 Spelling and Word Division

To many writers, the English language seems riddled with exceptions to spelling rules. Yet most words conform to specific guidelines, and even the exceptions can be categorized for easy reference. The guidelines in this section explain how to spell most regular and many troublesome words. Appendix D starting on page 137 provides a list of frequently misspelled words. Remember that the best guide to correct spelling is an updated dictionary.

## Spelling Guidelines

### Prefixes

A *prefix* added at the beginning of a word changes its meaning. However, the prefix does not change the spelling of that word. Most prefixes are added without using a hyphen.

    mis + step = misstep
    im + memorial = immemorial
    un + burden = unburden
    over + enthusiastic = overenthusiastic
    pre + formed = preformed
    in + tolerable = intolerable
    non + food = nonfood
    re + draw = redraw

Exceptions: the prefixes *ex-, self-, all-* are always used with a hyphen when they are joined to nouns.

    ex + prizefighter = ex-prizefighter
    self + awareness = self-awareness
    all + inclusive = all-inclusive

A hyphen is used when the prefix is joined to a proper noun or adjective.

    non + English = non-Engish
    pro + American = pro-American

A hyphen is used when the resulting word might be confused with a similar word of different meaning, or when the word might be confusing to the eye.

re + creation = re-creation (not recreation)
re + emphasize = re-emphasize
sub + subheading = sub-subheading

Prefixes show how many words and terms English has borrowed from Greek, Latin, and French. Following is a list of the common prefixes used in English along with their meanings.

| *Prefix* *(Old English)* | *Meaning* | *Example* |
|---|---|---|
| a- | in, on, of, up, to | arise, awake |
| be- | around, about, away | behead, bedevil |
| for- | away, off, from | forsake, forwarn |
| mis- | badly, poorly, not | misspell, mistake |
| over- | above, excessively | overextend, oversee |
| un- | not, reverse of | untidy, unnatural |

| *Prefix* *(Latin and Latin-French)* | *Meaning* | *Example* |
|---|---|---|
| ab-, a-, abs- | from, off, away | absent, abscond |
| ante- | before | antechamber, anteroom |
| bi- | two | biweekly, bisect |
| circum- | around | circumspect |
| col-, com-, con-, co-, cor- | with, together | collide, companion, congregate, coexist, correlate |
| contra- | against | contradict, controversial |
| de- | away, from, off, down | decline, depart |
| dif-, dis- | away, off, opposing | disagree, differ |
| e-, ef-, ex- | away, from, out | efface, exit |
| im-, in- | in, into, within | immerse, include |
| il-, im-, in-, ir- | not | illegal, immoral, inescapable, irreverent |
| inter- | among, between | intercept, interstate |
| intro-, intra- | inward, within | introduce, intrastate |
| non- | not | nonclinical, nonessential |
| post- | after, following | postscript, postoperative |
| pre- | before | preceding, prevent |
| pro- | forward, in place of, favoring | proceed, pronoun, pro-Canadian |
| re- | back, backward, again | recede, recur, reduce |
| retro- | back, backward | retroactive, retrojets |
| semi- | half | semicircle, semimonthly |
| sub-, suf-, sum-, sup-, sus- | under, beneath | suburb, suffuse, summon, .support, suspicion |
| super- | over, above, extra | supervise, superfluous |
| trans- | across, beyond | transport, transnational |
| ultra- | beyond, excessively | ultraviolet, ultramodern |

| Prefix (Greek) | Meaning | Example |
| --- | --- | --- |
| a- | lacking, without | amoral, atheist |
| anti- | against, opposing | antismoking, antithesis |
| apo- | from, away | apology |
| cata- | down, away, thoroughly | cataclysm, catacomb |
| dia- | through, across, apart | diameter, dialogue |
| epi- | at, on, over, among, beside | epidemic, epigraph |
| eu- | good, pleasant | euphoria, eulogy |
| hemi- | half | hemisphere |
| hyper- | excessive, over | hyperactive, hypertension |
| hypo- | under, beneath | hypodermic, hypotension |
| para- | beside, beyond | parallel, paradox |
| peri- | around | perimeter, peripheral |
| pro- | before | prognosis, progress |
| syl-, sym-, syn-, sys- | together, with | syllable, sympathy, synthesis, systematic |

## Suffixes

A *suffix* is added to the end of the word. In many cases, the spelling of the word does not change.

    sly + ly = slyly
    awkward + ness = awkwardness
    work + able = workable

The suffix *-elect,* however, is always used with a hyphen.

    secretary + elect = secretary-elect
    president + elect = president-elect

There are several instances in which the spelling of the root word does change when a suffix is added. The following guidelines categorize these changes.

**Final *y* as a Long *e* Sound**   If the final *y* of a word represents a long *e* sound, then the final *y* changes to *i* before adding the suffix *-ness* or *-ly.*

    merry + ly = merrily
    dizzy + ness = dizziness

**Final *y* Preceded by a Consonant**   With words that end in *y* and are preceded by a consonant, change the *y* to *i* before any suffix not beginning with *i.*

    sunny + er = sunnier
    happy + ly = happily (but *hurry + ing = hurrying*)

**Final *e* Before a Suffix Beginning with a Vowel** The final *e* is dropped before a suffix that begins with a vowel.

   dare + ing = daring
   sale + able = salable

The only exception to this rule is when the final *e* must be retained to maintain a soft *c* or *g* sound in the word.

   notice + able = noticeable
   courage + ous = courageous

**Final *e* Before a Suffix Beginning with a Consonant** Keep the final *e* when adding a suffix that begins with a consonant.

   use + ful = useful
   care + less = careless

There are a few exceptions to this rule:

   true + ly = truly (but *sincere + ly = sincerely*)
   argue + ment = argument

**Final *e* with the Suffix *-ment*** When the final *e* in a word is preceded by two consonants, drop the final *e* and add the suffix.

   acknowledge + ment = acknowledgment
   judge + ment = judgment

When the final *e* in a word is preceded by a vowel and a consonant, keep the final *e* and add the suffix.

   manage + ment = management

**Double Final Consonant Before a Suffix Beginning with a Vowel** The final consonant of a word is doubled when 1) the word has only one syllable, 2) the accent falls on the last syllable of the word (*prefer*), or 3) the word ends in a single consonant preceded by a single vowel.

   drag + ed = dragged
   sit + ing = sitting
   omít + ing = omitting
   occúr + ed = occurred
   prefér + ing = preferring (but *préferable)*
   contról + able = controllable

**Single Final Consonant Before a Suffix**   The final consonant remains single if the word is accented on the first syllable; if the final consonant is already double it remains double.

tárget + ed = targeted
cáncel + ing = canceling
tell + ing = telling
pull + ed = pulled

**Words Ending in Hard *c* Sound**   For words ending in a hard *c* sound, add *k* before suffixes *-in, -ed,* and *-y.*

panic + y = panicky
picnic + ing = picnicking
traffic + ed = trafficked
mimic + ing = mimicking

**Suffixes *-sede, -ceed, -cede***   Only one word in English ends in *-sede.*

super + sede = supersede

Only three words in English end in *-ceed.*

exceed   proceed   succeed

All other words with similar sounds end in *-cede.*

precede   recede   secede   concede   accede

**Suffixes *-able* and *-ible***   The suffixes *-able* and *-ible* sound alike and mean nearly the same things such as "capable of being" and "worthy of being." They are added to verbs and nouns to form adjectives.

irritate + able = irritable
permission + ible = permissible

There is a handy rule of thumb for knowing when to use *-able* or *-ible* that works for most words. When a related word can be formed ending in *-ation,* then *-able* is the correct suffix. When a related word can be formed ending in *-ion* or *-ive,* then *-ible* is correct.

dur*ation* = dur*able*
irrit*ation* = irrit*able*
repress*ion* = repress*ible*
permiss*ion* = permiss*ible*

If a word is not in the dictionary, it is spelled with *-able*.

When the suffix *-able* is added to a verb ending in *e*, the final *e* is dropped unless preceded by a *c* or *g*.

desire + able = desirable

use + able = usable

notice + able = noticeable

knowledge + able = knowledgeable

**Suffixes *-ant* and *-ent*, *-ance* and *-ence***   The four suffixes *-ant*, *-ent*, *-ance*, and *-ence* are added to change verbs to nouns and adjectives.

attend + ant = attendant

insist + ent = insistent

attend + ance = attendance

insist + ence = insistence

Unfortunately, there is no rule for knowing when to use which suffix. Memorize the spellings of words with these endings. However, if the word you wish to spell is not in the dictionary, use *-ant* or *-ance*.

**Suffixes *-er* and *-or***   The suffixes *-er* and *-or* sound alike and both mean *one who*. Some words are spelled with either ending.

act + or = actor

drive + er = driver

visit + or = visitor

speak + er = speaker

advise + or = advisor

advise + er = adviser

*-Er* is more common and is added to all new words in English. *-Or* occurs mainly with Latin root words, particularly legal terms, and is no longer added to words in English. If a word cannot be found in the dictionary, use the *-er* suffix.

**Suffixes *-ize* and *-ise***   The suffixes *-ize* and *-ise* are added to adjectives and nouns to make verbs. The suffix *-ize* is used in American English while the suffix *-ise* is British.

legal + ize = legalize

custom + ize = customize

critic + ize = criticize

Some words use either suffix as an ending, while others are spelled only with *-ise*.

mesmer + ise = mesmerise

mesmer + ize = mesmerize

advise   exercise   enterprise   disguise   chastise

If a word is not in the dictionary, use the *-ize* suffix as the correct ending.

Suffixes, like prefixes, have been added to English from several sources. Following is a list of the most common suffixes for nouns, adjectives, and verbs from Old English, Greek, Latin, and French along with their meanings.

| Noun Suffixes (Old English) | Meaning | Examples |
|---|---|---|
| -dom | state, rank, condition | kingdom, wisdom, martyrdom |
| -er | doer, maker | writer, teacher |
| -hood | state, condition | statehood, brotherhood |
| -ness | quality, state | hardness, likeness |

| Noun Suffixes (Latin, French, Greek) | Meaning | Examples |
|---|---|---|
| -age | process, state, rank | peerage, passage |
| -ance, -ancy | act, condition, fact | vigilance, vacancy |
| -ard, -art | one that does (in excess) | coward, braggart |
| -ate | office, rank | delegate, potentate |
| -ation | action, state, result | occupation, starvation |
| -cy | state, condition | deliquency, accuracy |
| -ee | one receiving action | retiree, employee |
| -eer | doer, worker at | engineer, mountaineer |
| -ence | act, condition, fact | evidence, sentence |
| -er | doer, native of | financier, baker |
| -ery | skill, action, collection | surgery, cookery |
| -ess | feminine | princess, lioness |
| -et, -ette | little, feminine | islet, majorette |
| -ion | action, result, state | union, conclusion |
| -ism | act, manner, doctrine | baptism, barbarism, feminism |
| -ist | doer, believer | plagiarist, socialist |
| -ition | action, state, result | sedition, expedition |
| -ity | state, quality, condition | civility, rarity |
| -ment | means, result, action | embarrassment, fulfillment |
| -or | doer, office, action | actor, juror |
| -ry | condition, practice, collection | archery, jewelry |
| -tion | action, condition | delegation, destruction |
| -tude | quality, state, result | multitude, fortitude |
| -ty | quality, state | witty, beauty |
| -ure | act, result, means | culture, ligature |
| -y | result, action, quality | arty, jealousy, handy |

| Adjective Suffixes (Old English) | Meaning | Examples |
|---|---|---|
| -en | made of, like | silken, golden |
| -ful | full of, marked by | thoughtful, careful |
| -ish | suggesting, like | prudish, childish |
| -less | lacking, without | thankless, hopeless |
| -like | like, similar | catlike, dreamlike |
| -ly | like, of the nature of | heavily, friendly |
| -some | apt to, showing | worrisome, tiresome |
| -ward | in the direction of | forward, downward |
| -y | showing, suggesting | heavy, wavy, rocky |

| Adjective Suffixes (Foreign) | Meaning | Examples |
|---|---|---|
| -able | able, likely | workable, likeable |
| -ate | having, showing | animate, duplicate |
| -escent | becoming, growing | obsolescent |
| -esque | in the style of, like | statuesque, picturesque |
| -fic | making, causing | terrific |
| -ible | able, likely, fit | producible, edible |
| -ose | marked by, given to | bellicose, comatose |
| -ous | marked by, given to | wondrous, religious |

| Adjective/Noun Suffixes | Meaning | Examples |
|---|---|---|
| -al | doer, pertaining to | ritual, autumnal |
| -an | one belonging to, pertaining to | American, human |
| -ant | actor, agent, showing | servant |
| -ary | belonging to, one connected with | functionary, adversary |
| -ent | doing, showing, actor | agent, confident |
| -ese | of a place or style | Japanese, journalese |
| -ian | pertaining to, one belonging to | reptilian, Sicilian |
| -ic | dealing with, caused by, person or thing, | scientific, epidemic |
| -ile | marked by, one marked by | senile, juvenile |
| -ine | marked by, dealing with, one marked by | divine, feline, marine |
| -ite | formed, showing, one marked by | Muscovite, favorite, composite |
| -ory | doing, pertaining to, place or thing for | accessory, observatory |

| Verb Suffix (Old English) | Meaning | Example |
|---|---|---|
| -en | cause to be, become | enliven, awaken |

| Verb Suffixes (Foreign) | Meaning | Examples |
|---|---|---|
| -ate | become, form, treat | formulate, agitate |
| -esce | become, grow, continue | convalesce, acquiesce |
| -fy | make, cause, cause to have | fortify, glorify |
| -ish | do, make, perform | finish, distinguish |
| -ize | make, cause to be | mobilize, sterilize |

# Plurals

**Regular Nouns**   The plural of most nouns is formed by adding *s:*

eagle   eagles

minister   ministers

record   records

**Irregular Nouns**   For most irregular nouns, the spelling changes to form the plural. Because the spelling changes do not follow any general rule, the forms must be memorized.

| Singular | Plural |
|---|---|
| child | children |
| goose | geese |
| man | men |
| mouse | mice |
| woman | women |

Some irregular nouns keep the same form for both singular and plural.

| Singular | Plural |
|---|---|
| deer | deer |
| sheep | sheep |
| species | species |

**Nouns Ending in *s, ss, z, sh, ch, x***   For nouns ending in *s, ss, z, sh, ch,* and *x*, add *es* to form the plural.

| | | | | |
|---|---|---|---|---|
| address | addresses | | fez | fezes |
| box | boxes | | gas | gases |
| buzz | buzzes | | kiss | kisses |
| dish | dishes | | watch | watches |

**Nouns Ending in *y*** For nouns ending in *y* preceded by a consonant, change the *y* to *i* and add *es*. For nouns ending in *y* preceded by a vowel, simply add *s*.

*Nouns ending in y preceded by a consonant*

| | | | |
|---|---|---|---|
| category | categories | secretary | secretaries |
| currency | currencies | territory | territories |

*Nouns ending in y preceded by a vowel*

| | | | |
|---|---|---|---|
| delay | delays | relay | relays |
| holiday | holidays | Wednesday | Wednesdays |

**Nouns Ending in *o*** For nouns ending in *o* preceded by a consonant, add *s* or *es*. If the *o* is preceded by a vowel, add *s*.

*Nouns ending in o preceded by a consonant*

| | |
|---|---|
| hero | heroes |
| potato | potatoes |
| solo | solos |
| tomato | tomatoes |
| zero | zeroes |

*Nouns ending in o preceded by a vowel*

| | |
|---|---|
| radio | radios |
| stereo | stereos |
| studio | studios |

All musical and literary terms ending in *o* add *s* to form the plural.

| | | | |
|---|---|---|---|
| oratorio | oratorios | rondo | rondos |
| piano | pianos | soprano | sopranos |

**Nouns Ending in *f* or *fe*** Many nouns ending in *f* or *fe* simply add *s* to form the plural. However, some nouns change the *f* to *v* and add *es*.

*Add s*

| | | | |
|---|---|---|---|
| chief | chiefs | dwarf | dwarfs |

*Change f or fe to v and add s or es*

| | | | |
|---|---|---|---|
| half | halves | self | selves |
| knife | knives | wife | wives |
| life | lives | wolf | wolves |

**Compound Nouns as One Word**   Compound nouns written as one word and ending in *s*, *sh*, *ch*, or *x* form the plural by adding *es*. In all other cases, the plural is formed by simply adding *s*.

*Compound nouns adding es*

lockbox    lockboxes                              toothbrush    toothbrushes

*Compound nouns adding s*

firefighter    firefighters                       mainframe    mainframes

**Compound Nouns as Two Words**   The plural of compound nouns written as two or more words is formed by adding *s* to the main word.

| | |
|---|---|
| chairman of the board | chairmen of the boards |
| editor in chief | editors in chief |
| notary public | notary publics |
| vice president | vice presidents |

**Hyphenated Compound Nouns**   Hyphenated compound nouns are made plural either by adding *s* to the main word or, if there is no main word, adding *s* to the end of the compound.

*Adding s to the main word*

| | |
|---|---|
| ex-governor | ex-governors |
| passer-by | passers-by |
| president-elect | presidents-elect |
| son-in-law | sons-in-law |

*Adding s to the end of the compound*

| | |
|---|---|
| grown-up | grown-ups |
| start-up | start-ups |
| trade-in | trade-ins |
| write-in | write-ins |

**Foreign Words**   Some foreign words form the plurals as they would in the original language.

| *Singular* | *Plural* |
|---|---|
| alumna (female) | alumnae |
| alumnus (male) | alumni |
| basis | bases |
| crisis | crises |
| datum | data |
| tableau | tableaux |

Other foreign words form the plural either as they do in the original language or by adding *s* or *es* as in English. When in doubt about the preferred form, consult a dictionary.

| *Singular* | *Foreign Plural* | *English Plural* |
|------------|------------------|------------------|
| appendix   | appendices       | appendixes       |
| formula    | formulae         | formulas         |
| index      | indices          | indexes          |

**Numbers, Letters, Words, Symbols**    The plural of numbers, letters, words, and symbols is formed by adding apostrophe *s* to the term.

| | |
|---|---|
| three 5's | two &'s and three #'s |
| use l's and m's | yes's and no's |

## The *i* and *e* Rules

Use *i* before *e*, except after *c* for the long *e* sound in a word.

*i before e—long e sound*

| | |
|---|---|
| believe | relieve |
| grievance | retrieve |
| piece | thief |

The exception to this rule are the words *either, neither, leisure, seized,* and *weird.*

Use *e* before *i* after *c* for the long *e* sound in a word.

*e before i after c—long e sound*

| | |
|---|---|
| ceiling | receipt |
| deceive | receive |

Use *e* before *i* when the sound in the word is not long *e*.

*e before i—no long e sound*

| | |
|---|---|
| eight | neighbor |
| freight | weigh |
| height | weight |

# Word Division

Like spelling rules, the rules for word division may seem arbitrary. Actually, they follow specific guidelines. The following rules explain the basics of properly dividing words. A good dictionary is the best guide for dividing words correctly.

## General Rules

Following are two general rules for word division.

**1. Avoid dividing words at the end of more than three successive lines.**

Avoid: We came into the conference hall late but man-
aged to find our seat-
ing arrangements before
the first speaker began.

Better: We came into the conference hall late but man-
aged to find our seating
arrangements before the
first speaker began.

**2. Avoid dividing a word at the end of a page or at the end of a paragraph.**

## Syllables and Word Division

Words are divided only between syllables. As a result, one-syllable words such as *trough, while,* and *their* are never divided.

Each syllable in word division must contain a vowel; therefore, most contractions cannot be divided.

con-trol   (not *con-tr-ol*)
hy-drau-lic   (not *hy-dr-au-lic*)

couldn't   (not *could-n't*)
isn't   (not *is-n't*)

When a word is divided, there must be more than one letter on the first line and more than two letters on the second line.

|  |  |
|---|---|
| *Incorrect:* | He apologized to Ethel most **sincere-ly.** |
| *Correct:* | He apologized to Ethel most **sin-cerely.** |
| *Incorrect:* | She told reporters that all her **jewel-ry** had been stolen from its case. |
| *Correct:* | She told reporters that all her **jew-elry** had been stolen from its case. |
| *Incorrect:* | "Look at this letter; it's full of **e-rasures.**" |
| *Correct:* | "Look at this letter; it's full of **era-sures.**" |
| *Incorrect:* | He's not sick. He's suffering from **a-pathy.** |
| *Correct:* | He's not sick. He's suffering from **ap-athy.** |

## Single-Letter Syllables

A single-letter syllable will always be a vowel. Generally, a single-letter syllable within a word should be left with the first part of the word and not carried over to the second line.

bus-i-ness = busi-ness (not *bus-iness*)
ox-y-gen = oxy-gen (not *ox-ygen*)
sep-a-rate = sepa-rate (not *sep-arate*)

When two single-letter syllables occur together in a word, divide the word between the single-letter syllables.

grad-u-a-tion = gradu-ation   (not *grad-uation*)
in-sin-u-a-tion = insinu-ation   (not *insin-uation*)

When the single-letter syllable *a, i,* or *u* is followed by the final syllable *ble, bly,* or *cal,* join the two end syllables and carry them over to the next line.

cler-i-cal = cler-ical (not *cleri-cal*)
de-pend-a-ble = depend-able (not *dependa-ble*)
in-vinc-i-ble = invinc-ible (not *invinci-ble*)

## Final and Double Consonants

If a final consonant preceded by a vowel is doubled before adding a suffix, divide the word between the two consonants.

plan + ing = planning = plan-ning
set + ing = setting = set-ting
win + ing = winning = win-ning

If the root word ends in a double consonant before the suffix is added, divide the word between the *root word and the suffix.*

assess + ing = assessing = assess-ing
tell + ing = telling = tell-ing

A word should never be divided between two or three consonants pronounced as one.

catch-ing   (not *cat-ching*)
cush-ion   (not *cus-hion*)
leath-ery   (not *leat-hery*)

## Hyphenated Words

Divide hyphenated words and compound hyphenated words only at the hyphen that connects them.

self-assessment = self- assessment   (not *self-assess- ment*)

clearing-house = clearing- house   (not *clear- ing-house*)

client-oriented approach = client- oriented approach   (not *client-or- iented ap- proach*)

## Proper Names

Avoid dividing a person's name or any proper name. Separate titles, initials, or degrees from names only when it is unavoidable.

| *Avoid:* | Mrs. Joan Cunning-ham | *Better:* | Mrs. Joan Cunningham |
|---|---|---|---|
| | Ms. Angela Sortino | | Ms. Angela Sortino |
| | George Watson, Ph.D. | | George Watson, Ph.D. |

## Figures and Abbreviations

In general, avoid dividing figures and abbreviations. However, if parts of an address or a date must be separated, use the following guidelines.

*Dividing Addresses*

| *Avoid:* | 15 Water Street | *Better:* | 15 Water Street |
|---|---|---|---|
| | 557 West Lock-port | | 557 West Lockport |
| | 1903 - 71st Avenue | | 1903 - 71st Avenue |
| | New York, New York | | New York, New York |

*Dividing Dates*

| *Avoid:* | August 20, 1976 | *Better:* | August 20, 1976 |
|---|---|---|---|
| | September 15, 19-55 | | September 15, 1955 |

# Part Two:
# *Style*
# *Considerations*

Although "style" in writing is a highly individual matter, some general rules and guidelines have been developed over the years to produce more precise, lively, and informative prose. This part discusses sentence structure and patterns; brevity, clarity, and accuracy; and gender-inclusive language.

# 2.1 Sentences

In composing sentences, many writers end up with one of two extremes: short, choppy sentences or long, complex ones. Thoughts may be expressed in brief, staccato statements that leave the reader short of breath. Or a sentence may start out with one idea and add a qualifier here, a modifier there, an incidental fact or two. By the time the sentence is finished, it has become a verbal maze for the reader.

Writing clear, informative sentences is as much art as it is the skilled use of grammatical rules. The guidelines presented in this section explain how to compose sentences that convey the intended meaning and capture the reader's interest.

## Using Sentence Patterns

The following guidelines show how to use various sentence patterns to express ideas.

**1. Use clarity and meaning as the criteria for good sentences.**

Each sentence should say *something* about the central idea of its paragraph without saying *too much or too little*. Build the reader's understanding key step by key step. In the following example, the writer has presented the facts in undersized bites, creating an awkward style.

> *Choppy:* Hank sailed around the world. He did it alone in a 30-foot sailboat. His radio was his only link with the outside world. He caught fish for his meals and trapped rainwater to drink. His solitary journey took 168 days.

In the second example, the writer has committed the opposite fault of trying to say everything in one sentence.

> *Complex:* Hank sailed around the world in 168 days in a 30-foot sailboat with only a radio to connect him to the outside world and only fresh fish and rainwater to keep his provisions stocked.

Both examples express complete thoughts, but the clarity and meaning of the information is muddled by the way it is presented. What facts in the story are more important than the others? Is there some way of ordering the material so the reader has a sense of key facts versus merely interesting ones?

In the following revision, the writer has ordered the information and used clarity and meaning as the criteria for sentence construction.

> *Revised:*    Hank completed his record solo voyage around in the world in a mere 168 days. He made the journey in a 30-foot sailboat, whose short-wave radio served as his only link with the outside world. He kept his provisions stocked by catching fish and trapping rainwater to drink.

In the revised version, the reader is given not only the necessary information but also some idea of its importance and meaning.

### 2. Include only one to two ideas in each sentence.

Many times writers will trap themselves into long, involved sentences because they are free associating rather than carefully constructing their thoughts. A series of ideas in one sentence rushes the reader too quickly through the material. Before one idea has time to settle, another crowds it out of the way. Such sentences can be separated into shorter, simpler constructions.

> *Original:*    Our study on the impact of the Environmental Pollution Act revealed that water quality has improved by an average of 35 percent in 14 states but toxic waste is still a major concern among most residents since this issue has not been addressed in any systematic way because of confusion within the Environmental Protection Agency about how to enforce the regulations.

The conjunctions such as *and, but, since,* and *because* often signal where a new sentence can begin. The preceding paragraph can be rewitten as follows:

> *Revised:*    Our study on the impact of the Environmental Pollution Act revealed that water quality has improved by an average of 35 percent in 14 states. Toxic waste, however, is still a major concern among most residents. This issue has not been addressed systematically, because the Environmental Protection Agency has not set guidelines on enforcing toxic waste regulations.

In the revision, each sentence contains only one or two ideas. The reader has time to absorb the information in each sentence before going on to the next one.

**3. Vary sentence patterns to avoid the monotonous use of any particular construction.**

A writer may unconsciously adopt one type of sentence pattern throughout a paragraph. A short, staccato pattern can mimic a cool, unemotional tone. On the other hand, if all the sentences begin with subordinate clauses, it may appear that the paragraph is taking a circular route to the main point.

The English sentence can be composed in a variety of ways to add interest and liveliness. The four basic sentence constructions—simple, compound, complex, and compound-complex—can be combined in paragraphs to help the reader move from one idea to the next.

To review the four basic sentence patterns:

*Simple:* **I would like to go home.** (an independent clause with no subordinate clause)

*Compound:* **I'm not feeling well, and I would like to go home.** (two or more independent clauses but no subordinate clauses)

*Complex:* **Because I'm not feeling well, I would like to go home.** (an independent clause and one or more subordinate clauses)

*Compound-complex:* **I'm not feeling well because I ate six taffy apples, and I would like to go home.** (two or more independent clauses and one or more subordinate clauses; the subordinate clause is underscored)

The following example is written exclusively in short, simple sentences. The revision uses complex and compound sentences to vary the constructions. Read the two versions aloud. Notice how the change in rhythm affects the reader's perception and feelings about the material.

*Monotonous:* Lawrence entered Mecca through the south gate. The sun was high overhead. Its brutal heat struck him speechless. Pilgrims blocked the narrow streets and alleyways. His guide found him lodgings near the mosque. He would be contacted soon by the Mecca agent. He had only two days left to complete his mission.

*Varied:* Lawrence entered Mecca through the south gate. The sun was high overhead, and its brutal heat struck him speechless. In every section of the city, pilgrims blocked the narrow streets and alleyways. His guide found him lodgings near the mosque, and Lawrence settled in to wait for the Mecca agent. With only two days left to complete his mission, Lawrence hoped the man would arrive soon.

In the next example, the writer uses introductory subordinate clauses for all sentences. Read aloud the two versions and notice how varying the sentence structure changes the rhythm and tone of the text.

*Monotonous:*   After waiting 24 hours, Lawrence knew that something was wrong. Because he had used only embassy couriers to carry his messages, he suspected a security leak among the embassy staff. Even if his suspicions were wrong, it was evident that somewhere along the line the message had been intercepted. Although his orders said to stay in Mecca, Lawrence left the city that night.

*Varied:*   After waiting 24 hours, Lawrence knew that something was wrong. He had used only embassy couriers to carry his messages to the Mecca contact. Was there a security leak among the embassy staff? His suspicions might be groundless, but somewhere along the line the message had been intercepted. Although his orders said to stay in Mecca, Lawrence left the city that night.

Experiment with various sentence patterns by recasting sentences in the four basic forms. Use the examples below as guides for rewriting sentences. Notice that by altering the patterns, different facts in the sentence can be stressed.

*Simple:*   He reached Akaba and learned the Mecca contact had disappeared.

*Compound:*   He reached Akaba, and headquarters told him the Mecca contact had disappeared.

*Complex:*   When he reached Akaba, headquarters told him the Mecca contact, who had been under surveillance, had disappeared.

*Compound-complex:*   When he reached Akaba, headquarters told him that the Mecca agent had disappeared, and all his contacts had been arrested.

# 2.2 Brevity

It has been said that "brevity is the soul of wit." Many sentences are inflated with wordy phrases or expressions that add nothing to the meaning or impact of what is being said. The following guidelines explain how to make written messages more concise.

**1. In general, avoid the phrases *there is* and *there are*.**
Rewrite sentences using more active verbs.

> *Avoid:* There are three reasons for Marty's odd behavior.
> *Better:* I can tell you three reasons for Marty's odd behavior.
> Three reasons exist for Marty's odd behavior.

> *Avoid:* Whenever it rains, there is water in the basement.
> *Better:* Whenever it rains, water collects in the basement.
> Whenever it rains, the basement floods.

**2. Try to condense clauses beginning with *which, that,* or *who* into fewer words.**

> *Poor:* The visitor, who was from England, brought us a package that was square and heavy.
> *Better:* The English visitor brought us a square, heavy package.

> *Poor:* The building, which was 24 stories, collapsed during the earthquake that struck last night.
> *Better:* The 24-story building collapsed during last night's earthquake.

**3. Strike out the article *the* wherever possible to improve the flow and readability of sentences.**

~~The~~ shore lights reflected in Santiago Bay made the hotels and ~~the~~ casinos appear to float above the water.

~~The~~ bears come out in ~~the~~ spring and look for ~~the~~ honey that ~~the~~ bees have guarded all winter.

The importance of *the* can be determined by crossing it out and reading the sentence for meaning. If the sentence is less clear, restore the article.

## 4. Eliminate wordy and redundant phrases and expressions.

| | |
|---|---|
| *Avoid:* | The birds are bright yellow **in color.** |
| *Better:* | The birds are bright yellow. |

| | |
|---|---|
| *Avoid:* | Of course, I'm only thinking **on a theoretical basis.** |
| *Better:* | Of course, I'm only thinking theoretically. |

| | |
|---|---|
| *Avoid:* | **In the vast majority of cases,** chicken pox is not fatal. |
| *Better:* | In most cases, chicken pox is not fatal. |

| | |
|---|---|
| *Avoid:* | **The reason** I don't want you to go is **that** the Amazon is no place for a summer vacation. |
| *Better:* | I don't want you to go, because the Amazon is no place for a summer vacation. |

Following is a list of wordy phrases commonly used by many writers. Compare them with their more concise alternatives. Change the wordy phrases wherever they appear.

| *Wordy* | *Concise* |
|---|---|
| at this point in time | at this time |
| consensus of opinion | consensus |
| meet together | meet |
| blend together | blend |
| during the course of | during |
| few in number | few |
| personal in manner | personal |
| on a weekly basis | weekly |
| refer back to | refer to |
| square in shape | square |
| until such time as | until |
| due to the fact that | because |
| very necessary | necessary |
| in spite of the fact that | although |
| engaged in a study of | studying |
| depreciates in value | depreciates |
| opening gambit | gambit (a gambit is an opening move in chess) |
| this is a subject that | this subject |
| the fact that she had come | her coming |
| in a hasty manner | hastily |

Redundant words and expressions repeat or rephrase what has been said in a sentence. They occur frequently in writing and should be deleted. Redundant expressions are easy to spot once you learn how and where to look for them.

| | |
|---|---|
| *Avoid:* | To find his mistake, he had to retrace the steps **he had taken before.** (*Retrace* means to go back over the steps or path taken before. The clause in boldface is unnecessary.) |
| *Better:* | To find his mistake, he had to retrace his steps. |

| | |
|---|---|
| *Avoid:* | **In the month of** June, we traveled through **the states of** Georgia, North Carolina, and Virginia. |
| *Better:* | In June, we traveled through Georgia, North Carolina, and Virginia. |

# 2.3 Clarity

Clear writing involves getting the words just right. Choose the best words to express your ideas in the best manner possible. Do not assume that written material is clear to the reader. This section presents guidelines for clear writing.

## Keep the Words Fresh

Writing should be free of jargon, buzz words, and cliches. Such words and phrases come easily to mind yet convey little real information. Delete them and substitute more precise words.

### Jargon

Jargon refers to specialized terms of a profession that the general reader probably would not understand. Rewrite sentences to eliminate jargon or make sure that all terms are defined.

*Avoid:* The computer **downloaded** all the data to the printer, but we had to **exit** before the job was complete.

*Better:* The computer **sent** all the data to the printer, but we had to **stop** before the job was complete.

### Buzz Words

Buzz words are terms that come into fashion for a time and find their way into everyone's writing. They are often borrowed from various professions and adapted to general use. Eliminate buzz words and choose better words. Some of today's buzz words include the following:

| | | |
|---|---|---|
| on line | interactive | head honcho |
| input | bottom line | parameter |
| paradigm | interface | relevant |
| scenario | street smarts | at this point in time |
| viable | taxwise (or anything -wise) | impact on (as a verb) |

*Avoid:* I don't know how well Greg is going to **interface** with Linda. They haven't worked together before.

*Better:* I don't know how well Greg is going to **get along with** Linda. They haven't worked together before.

Some words and phrases from the legal field have been appropriated for general use—often inappropriately. Avoid using the following terms for everyday writing:

| | |
|---|---|
| aforementioned | per, as per |
| duly | pursuant to |
| herein | re (meaning *regarding*) |
| hereto | therein |
| herewith | whereas |
| notwithstanding the above (or afore-mentioned) | |

> *Avoid:* **Re** your letter of the 25th, we are sending you five memo pads **per** your order and enclosing the invoice **herein.**

> *Better:* We received your order, dated October 25, for five memo pads. Enclosed please find the memo pads and an invoice itemizing price and shipping costs.

## Cliches

Cliches are trite, worn-out expressions. While they are acceptable in conversation, they should be avoided in writing. Following are some common cliches:

| | |
|---|---|
| stiff as a board | slick as a whistle |
| oldies but goodies | keep your shirt on |
| mind-blowing | too good to be true |
| crying over spilt milk | getting in touch with |
| on the warpath | out of the frying pan |
| up to your ears | on the tip of my tongue |
| deader than a doornail | bigger than life |
| neat as a pin | needle in a haystack |
| pearls of wisdom | a stitch in time |

> *Avoid:* I think Helen is as **sound as a dollar** and **honest as the day is long,** but her thoughts on this issue are **off the wall.** I don't think her ideas will **hold up in the wash.**

> *Better:* I think Helen is sensible and honest, but her thoughts on this issue are not well reasoned. I don't think her ideas will hold up under scrutiny.

# Keep Words Specific and Concrete

The more abstract a word or phrase, the less people will understand exactly what is meant. Abstract terms are subject to considerable individual interpretation. For example, the terms *national security, quality education,* and *consumer interests* can mean widely different things to different people.

Concrete words, on the other hand, refer to something specific, often something that can be seen, heard, touched, tasted, or smelled. Their meaning is also more precise and less open to personal interpretation. Use concrete words as much as possible in writing. Although abstract words can be used for summarizing ideas and creating a framework for a discussion, ground the framework in tangible, concrete details.

| | |
|---|---|
| *Abstract:* | I think this story is **overly dramatic.** |
| *Concrete:* | I think this story relies too much on emotion, coincidence, and manipulation of characters. |
| *Abstract:* | The company's sales picture is **gloomy** this year. |
| *Concrete:* | The 25 percent drop in sales means we will probably not meet our objectives this year. |
| *Abstract:* | His tennis game is **off.** |
| *Concrete:* | His backstroke is weak, and he can't maintain his concentration. |

Many people also try to make their writing sound more formal or official by using abstract words instead of concrete ones.

| | |
|---|---|
| *Avoid:* | Please refrain from discarding litter items on the company grounds or in the company buildings. Use the litter receptacles placed throughout the plant for such purposes. Your cooperation in this matter is appreciated. |
| *Better:* | Please deposit all waste paper, aluminum cans, bottles, and other trash in the litter baskets. Help keep your grounds and building clean! We appreciate your cooperation. |

Vague or abstract words leave unanswered such questions as *What kind? How much? Which one? In what way?* By using concrete words, readers' questions are answered with specific information.

# Keep References Clear

When words are used to modify or refer to other words, make sure the reader can follow the intended train of thought. If references are used carelessly, some unintended humor may be provided.

> If you can't hang the clothes yourself, ask for help in hanging them from your mother.
>
> Our camp leader is over there—the stocky, red-haired man with a beach ball named Tom Robbins.

Such confusion can be avoided by following a few basic guidelines to keep references clear.

### 1. Keep modifiers close to the words they modify.

> *Poor:* The band played **three songs** during their tour **written by a 12-year-old girl.**
>
> *Better:* During their tour, the band played **three songs written by a 12-year-old girl.**

### 2. Place adverbs close to the words they modify.

Pay particular attention to placement of the adverb *only*. The reader should not have to guess at the sentence's meaning.

> *Incorrect:* I **only** wanted three hot dogs, not five.
>
> *Correct:* I wanted **only** three hot dogs, not five.

> *Poor:* The letter we **received recently managed** to upset everyone. (Is it *received recently* or *recently managed*?)
>
> *Better:* The letter we **recently received managed** to upset everyone.

### 3. Keep subject and verb together.

This arrangement helps the reader follow the thought and understand the sentence more easily.

> *Avoid:* **The white-pebble beach,** which had once been the site of a bloody battle in the sixteenth century when the Duke of Westmoreland and the Baron De Haviland had fought over Devonshire County, **had been deserted for two hundred years.**
>
> *Better:* **The white-pebble beach had been deserted for two hundred years.** Yet in the sixteenth century it had been the site of a bloody battle between the Duke of Westmoreland and Baron De Haviland. The prize was all of Devonshire County.

Often the solution to the problem of subject-verb placement is to break the sentence into two or more shorter sentences.

### 4.  Make sure that antecedents are clear.

Words such as *this, that, who, what, which* and *it* refer to the preceding noun or pronoun in the sentence or previous sentence. If the antecedents are not clear, the sentences will confuse the reader and may provide some unexpected humor.

> We will paint any car, any make for only $59.95. Our offer is good for this week only. Have your car painted before it expires!

The antecedent for *it* is *the offer,* not *the car.* But the reader must look twice at the sentence to determine the writer's true intention. Study the following examples.

> *Poor:*  I served avocados for lunch, **which** no one felt like eating. (Did no one feel like eating the avocados or the lunch?)
>
> *Better:*  I served avocados for lunch, but no one felt like eating them.
> No one felt like eating the avocados I served for lunch.
>
> *Poor:*  I dropped the jar, and pickles rolled all over the floor, under the table, and out into the hallway. **This** was not going to please my mother! (To what does *this* refer? Avoid using words that refer to an entire sentence or idea.)
>
> *Better:*  I dropped the jar and pickles rolled all over the floor, under the table, and out into the hallway. **This mess** was not going to please my mother!

A variety of methods can be used to correct confusing references. These include breaking one sentence into two or more, rearranging word order, restating the sentence, or filling in the missing reference.

# Keep Structures Parallel

Phrases and clauses in a series or within a sentence should be parallel; that is, they should have the same structure. In the following example, the writer begins with infinitive phrases, then changes to another structure at the end.

> We learned how to change a tire, to shift 16 gears, and once almost ran the truck off the road.

Once a parallel structure has been started, the reader expects it to continue. If the structure changes in midstream, readers will be confused. The preceding example should read as follows:

> We learned how **to change** a tire, **to shift** 16 gears, and **to keep** the truck from running off the road.

Look over the following examples. In some cases, the violation of parallel structure is not always obvious.

| | |
|---|---|
| *Incorrect:* | We sold jeans to **the** Spanish, **the** French, Italians, and Germans. |
| *Correct:* | We sold jeans to the Spanish, the French, the Italians, and the Germans. |
| | We sold jeans to the Spanish, French, Italians, and Germans. |

An article or preposition used in a series of terms must be used only before the first term or with all the terms.

Correlative conjunctions—such as *both, and; not, but; not only, but also;* and *either, or*—should be followed by the same grammatical structure. This rule is also true for any series introduced by *first, second, third,* and so on. The sentence may need to be rearranged to correct the problem.

| | |
|---|---|
| *Incorrect:* | The lecture was **both a tedious one and much too long.** |
| *Correct:* | The lecture was **both tedious and long.** |

| | |
|---|---|
| *Incorrect:* | It's not a time **for emotion but clear thinking.** |
| *Correct:* | It's not a time **for** emotion **but for** clear thinking. |

| | |
|---|---|
| *Incorrect:* | My reasons are **first,** the expedition is too dangerous and **second, that it is unnecessary.** |
| *Correct:* | My reasons are **first,** the expedition is too dangerous and **second, it is unnecessary.** |

Writers also violate parallel structure when they mix verb forms within a sentence.

I **have mowed** the lawn, **washed** the dog, **rescued** our hamster, and **went** to the store all in one day.

The verb form *went* is incorrect with the auxiliary verb *have.* The sentence can be rewritten as follows:

I **have mowed** the lawn, **washed** the dog, **rescued** our hamster, and **gone** to the store all in one day.

I **mowed** the lawn, **washed** the dog, **rescued** our hamster, and **went** to the store all in one day.

# 2.4 Accuracy

Accuracy is essential to good writing, whether the writing is an essay, a business report, a term paper, or a news article. The following guidelines help ensure that facts are correct.

**1. Double-check figures, dates, specifications, and other details.**

The motto is *When in doubt, check it out.* Make sure that any figures, dates, percentages, or other facts have been reported or copied accurately. Do not rely on memory.

**2. Be sure that all names, titles, and abbreviations are spelled properly.**

It can be considerably embarrassing to misspell proper names and titles of books, articles, plays, and the like. Find out whether abbreviations are spelled with periods, in all capitals, or with symbols such as ampersands.

**3. Verify the accuracy of direct quotations.**

Try to verify what people said and report their words accurately. In one instance, a reporter asked a political candidate the following question:

"Do you believe that we should do away with price supports for farmers and import more foreign commodities?"

The candidate replied, "Yes," and the reporter wrote in an article:

Candidate Brown said, "We should do away with price supports for farmers and import more foreign commodities."

The candidate had said nothing of the kind; he had merely responded to a question. The reporter should have written the following:

When asked if he favors eliminating price supports and importing more foreign commodities, the candidate replied, "Yes."

**4. Make sure that ideas are presented clearly.**

Clarity is essential to accuracy. Learn to spot muddled statements, abstract terms, nonparallel constructions, ambiguous expressions, and poor development of ideas.

Ask someone else to read what you have written. Chances are he or she will be able to point out weaknesses in your work that you cannot see.

**5.   Make sure your work is neat and legible.**

Sloppy handwriting, messy copy, or typographical errors can affect the accuracy of your work. Someone's name may be spelled incorrectly because you or a typist could not read your handwriting. A key figure may be blurred by a coffee stain, and you will have to search through your notes to find the correct number. Carelessness not only threatens accuracy but also can cost you considerable time and effort.

# 2.5 Gender-Inclusive Language

Events of the past two decades have made the public more aware of the sex bias in the English language. Use of sexist language can create confusion. For example, the use of the word *man* sometimes refers only to men and other times refers to both men and women. The conversion from sexist to gender-inclusive language can be made naturally and gracefully. In the following sections, guidelines are provided for using gender-inclusive nouns, pronouns, titles, and expressions.

## Nouns and Pronouns

**1. Try to use female and male pronouns only when referring to specific males and females.**

> *Avoid:* A good dentist reassures **his** patients.
>
> *Better:* Dr. Jacobs always reassures **his** patients.
> Dr. Jacobs always reassures **her** patients.

> *Avoid:* The elementary teacher has **her** hands full teaching today's children.
>
> *Better:* Ms. Hutton has **her** hands full teaching today's children.
> Mr. Hutton has **his** hands full teaching today's children.

**Note:** On occasion, use male and female paired pronouns *he or she, her or him, his or hers, etc.* instead of a male or female pronoun exclusively. This construction is particularly appropriate as a gentle reminder that both men and women make up the population that is being discussed. For example:

> *Avoid:* A good manager knows **his** staff.
>
> *Better:* A good manager knows **his or her** staff.

## 2. Make the nouns and pronouns plural.

*Avoid:*   The prudent **executive** should know where **his** money goes.

*Better:*   Prudent **executives** should know where **their** money goes.

*Avoid:*   The course is designed to help **your secretary** reach **her** full potential.

*Better:*   The course is designed to help **secretaries** reach **their** full potential.

**Note:** In informal writing and speech it is permissible to use the plural pronoun *they, them, their, theirs* with a singular noun or indefinite pronoun. However, use this construction sparingly.

*Avoid:*   Each manager knows **his** staff.

*(Sometimes) Better:*   Each manager knows **their** staff.

## 3. Use the first person *we*, second person *you*, or third person *one, each, those,* and so on, where appropriate.

*Avoid:*   **Man's** desire for excitement drives **him** to seek ever more daring challenges.

*Better:*   **Our** desire for excitement drives **us** to seek ever more daring challenges.

*Avoid:*   The **player** cannot throw the dice until **he** has drawn one card from the Community Chest pile.

*Better:*   **You** cannot throw the dice until **you** have drawn one card from the Community Chest pile.

*Avoid:*   For the **student** to grasp basic physics, **he** must understand the principles of energy, light, and matter.

*Better:*   To grasp basic physics, **one** must understand the principles of energy, light, and matter.

## 4. Reword sentences to eliminate the pronouns or replace them with gender-free words such as *a, an,* and *the*.

*Avoid:*   Each evening, the **night guard** makes **his** rounds of the building.

*Better:*   Each evening, the **night guard** patrols **the** building.

*Avoid:*   The **dietitian** prepares **her** nutritional analysis once a day.

*Better:*   The **dietitian** prepares **a** nutritional analysis once a day.

## 5. Use the passive voice occasionally instead of the active voice.

*Active:* Whenever an employee enters the building, **he should wear his** identification badge.

*Passive:* The identification badge **should be worn** whenever an employee enters the building.

## 6. To avoid sexist references, repeat the noun if it is separated from the second reference by a number of words.

*Avoid:* **The announcer** on a classical music station must know how to pronounce a wide range of foreign names and titles. **He** also must be able to read advertising and news copy.

*Better:* **The announcer** on a classical music station must know how to pronounce a wide range of foreign names and titles. **The announcer** also must be able to read advertising and news copy.

Substitute a different noun or pronoun such as *person* or *one* to avoid a monotonous repetition of the original noun.

*Monotonous:* **The inspector** checks all assembled products before they are shipped. **The inspector** reports any failures to the quality control manager, who passes on **the inspector's** data to the head office.

*Better:* **The inspector** checks all assembled products before they are shipped. **This person** reports any failures to the quality control manager, who passes on **the inspector's** data to the head office.

## Alternative Noun-Forms

English has accumulated many nouns that contain the word *-man* as a suffix or prefix: *businessman, chairman, congressman, man-hours.* These words can no longer be used to refer to both men and women. The following guidelines give alternatives to these terms.

**1. Avoid using *man* to refer to people as a group. Use the terms *humanity, human beings, persons, human race,* or *people* instead.**

| | |
|---|---|
| *Avoid:* | **Man (mankind)** is at a critical point in **his** history. |
| *Better:* | **Humanity (the human race)** is at a critical point in **its** history. |
| *Avoid:* | **Man** is a gregarious creature. |
| *Better:* | **People** are gregarious creatures. |

**2. Use *person* as the suffix or prefix instead of *man* where the usage would not create absurd constructions (for example, *personhole* cover; use *sewer cover* instead).**

| | |
|---|---|
| *Avoid:* | A **businessman** can fly half fare. |
| *Better:* | A **businessperson** can fly half fare. |
| *Avoid:* | The **chairman** draws up the agenda. |
| *Better:* | The **chairperson** draws up the agenda. |

**3. Use words other than *person* to replace *-man*.**

| | |
|---|---|
| *Avoid:* | The **policeman** gave me a ticket. |
| *Better:* | The **police officer** gave me a ticket. |
| *Avoid:* | Our **mailman** came early today. |
| *Better:* | Our **mail carrier** came early today. |
| *Avoid:* | This job will require 24 **man-hours.** |
| *Better:* | This job will require 24 **staff-hours.** |
| *Avoid:* | **Man-made** fabric is easier to clean. |
| *Better:* | **Synthetic** fabric is easier to clean. |

**4. Reword the sentence to avoid using *-man*.**

| | |
|---|---|
| *Avoid:* | **Freshman** students are always nervous. |
| *Better:* | **First-year** students are always nervous. |
| *Avoid:* | The team showed unusual **gamesmanship.** |
| *Better:* | The team **played the game shrewdly.** |

# Suffixes *-ess, -ette, -ix, -ienne/-ine*

In modern usage, the trend is to drop the suffixes that denote female forms of nouns: *poet, poetess; usher, usherette.* However, three forms are still widely used—*actress, hostess,* and *waitress.* Use the masculine and feminine forms when referring to both men and women.

> *Incorrect:*   Alice and Jim served as **hosts.**
>
> *Correct:*   Alice and Jim served as **hostess and host.**

## 1. Omit the following suffixes, which denote female when added to words.

*-ess ending*

| | | | |
|---|---|---|---|
| *Avoid:* | directress | *Better:* | director |
| | authoress | | author |
| | sculptress | | sculptor |

*-ette ending*

| | | | |
|---|---|---|---|
| *Avoid:* | usherette | *Better:* | usher |
| | drum majorette | | drum major |
| | bachelorette | | single |

*-ix ending*

| | | | |
|---|---|---|---|
| *Avoid:* | aviatrix | *Better:* | aviator |
| | executrix | | executor |

*-ienne/ine ending*

| | | | |
|---|---|---|---|
| *Avoid:* | comedienne | *Better:* | comedian |

## 2. Do not mix gender-inclusive and gender-determined words when pairing men and women.

> *Avoid:*   He is **chairman** of the Elks and she is **chairwoman** of the Junior League. As **chairmen,** they have little time at home.
>
> *Better:*   He is **chairman** of the Elks, and she is **chairwoman** of the Junior League. As **chairpersons,** they have little time at home.
>
> *Avoid:*   He is **chairperson** of the Elks, and she is **chairwoman** of the Junior League.
>
> *Better:*   He is **chairperson** of the Elks, and she is **chairperson** of the Junior League.
> He is **chairman** of the Elks, and she is **chairwoman** of the Junior League.

# Social Titles

The social titles *Mr., Mrs., Miss,* and *Ms.* can also be used in ways that do not perpetuate stereotypes. Following are some guidelines:

**1. Use *Mr.* for all men.**

**2. Use *Ms.* for all women when you do not know how they prefer to be addressed or do not know their marital status.**

**3. Use *Miss* or *Mrs.* when the woman herself uses these titles with her name.**

**4. Use a married woman's first name, not her husband's. For example, use Mrs. Dorothy Brandt, not Mrs. Harold Brandt, unless the woman specifies that she would like to be addressed by her husband's name.**

# Salutations

In writing business letters or direct mail messages, make sure the salutation includes all the readers who are likely to receive the message. Following are suggested ways to write gender-inclusive salutations.

**1. Avoid using *Dear Sir, Dear Gentlemen* or *My Dear Sirs*.** Use the following variations.

Ladies and Gentlemen:
Gentlepersons:
Dear Madames (Mesdames) and Sirs:
My Dear Sirs and Madames (Mesdames):
My Dear Sir or Madam (Madame or Sir):

**2. Address individuals by title or group name.**

| *Title* | *Group Name* |
|---|---|
| Dear Executive: | Dear Customer: |
| Dear Manager: | Dear Friend: |
| Dear Human Resources Director: | Dear Subscriber: |
| Dear Professor: | Dear Investor: |
| Dear Medical Writer: | To the Folks on Maple: |

# Occupational Titles

The U.S. Department of Labor in its *Dictionary of Occupational Titles* lists gender-inclusive titles for many occupations and positions such as the following:

| *Avoid* | *Revised* |
|---------|-----------|
| salesman | salesperson |
| craftsman | craftworker |
| draftsman | drafter |
| fireman | firefighter |
| watchman | guard, security officer |
| newsman | reporter, newspeople |
| foreman | supervisor |
| repairman | repairer |
| mailman | mail carrier, letter carrier |
| policeman | police, police officer |

See the *Dictionary of Occupational Titles* for a complete listing of titles and other business-related terms.

# Appendixes

# Appendix A. Principal Parts of Irregular Verbs

There are no fixed rules for forming the past tense and past and present participle of irregular verbs. It is necessary to memorize the forms and to keep a good dictionary handy. For reference, some of the most commonly used irregular verbs are listed below.

| Base Form | Past Tense | Past Participle | Present Participle |
|---|---|---|---|
| be | was | been | being |
| begin | began | begun | beginning |
| bite | bit | bitten | biting |
| blow | blew | blown | blowing |
| break | broke | broken | breaking |
| bring | brought | brought | bringing |
| burst | burst | burst | bursting |
| buy | bought | bought | buying |
| catch | caught | caught | catching |
| come | came | come | coming |
| do | did | done | doing |
| draw | drew | drawn | drawing |
| drink | drank | drunk | drinking |
| drive | drove | driven | driving |
| eat | ate | eaten | eating |
| fall | fell | fallen | falling |
| fight | fought | fought | fighting |
| flee | fled | fled | fleeing |
| fly | flew | flown | flying |
| forget | forgot | forgotten | forgetting |
| get | got | got/gotten | getting |
| give | gave | given | giving |
| go | went | gone | going |
| grow | grew | grown | growing |
| hang | hung/hanged | hung/hanged | hanging |
| hide | hid | hidden | hiding |
| know | knew | known | knowing |
| lay | laid | laid | laying |
| leave | left | left | leaving |
| lend | lent | lent | lending |
| lie | lay | lain | lying |
| lose | lost | lost | losing |
| pay | paid | paid | paying |

| *Base Form* | *Past Tense* | *Past Participle* | *Present Participle* |
|---|---|---|---|
| ride | rode | ridden | riding |
| ring | rang | rung | ringing |
| rise | rose | risen | rising |
| run | ran | run | running |
| see | saw | seen | seeing |
| set | set | set | setting |
| shake | shook | shaken | shaking |
| shine | shone | shone | shining |
| shrink | shrank | shrunk | shrinking |
| sit | sat | sat | sitting |
| speak | spoke | spoken | speaking |
| steal | stole | stolen | stealing |
| strike | struck | struck | striking |
| take | took | taken | taking |
| tear | tore | torn | tearing |
| throw | threw | thrown | throwing |
| wear | wore | worn | wearing |
| write | wrote | written | writing |

# Appendix B. Verb-Preposition Combinations

Verb-preposition combinations often defy attempts to categorize them under any logical system. As a result, the only solution is to learn through practice which prepositions are used with which verbs under what circumstances. Some of the more troublesome ones are presented here.

### agree with, agree to

*agree with*—concur in opinion (agree with a person)

I **agree with** Carl that we should operate tomorrow.

*agree to*—give assent (agree to an idea or thing)

I **agree to** an operation for my ulcer.

### angry with/at

*angry with/at*—enraged; *angry at* suggests a confrontation

She was **angry with** herself for sleeping late. The president was **angry at** the board for turning down his five-year program.

### answer to, answer for

*answer to*—be accountable to a person; respond to

You'll have to **answer to** the commission for your sales record. He's 4 years old and **answers to** the name "Fred."

*answer for*—be accountable for actions

You'll have to **answer for** your decision to abort the mission.

### on behalf of, in behalf of

*on behalf of*—as someone's representative

The lawyer will act **on behalf of** my brother to settle the estate.

*in behalf of*—in someone's interest

I set up a trust fund **in behalf of** my nephew.

### belong to, belong with

*belong to*—be a member of

They **belong to** the Secret Order of the Koala.

*belong with*—be classified or placed among

These flowers **belong with** the plants classified as grasses.

## capacity to, capacity of

> *capacity to*—capable of (used with a verb)
>
> She has the **capacity to** break the world's record for high jump.
>
> *capacity of*—content or volume (used with a measure)
>
> This silo has a **capacity of** 2,400 cubic feet and can hold 4,800 bushels of corn.

## compare to, compare with

> *compare to*—liken
>
> She **compared** my singing **to** Tina Turner's.
> "Shall I **compare** thee **to** a summer's day?"
>
> *compare with*—contrast for similarities and differences
>
> He **compared** the Russian military strength **with** the United States armed forces.

## concur in, concur with

> *concur in*—agree (in an opinion)
>
> The three judges **concurred in** their settlement of the case.
>
> *concur with*—agree (with another person)
>
> I must **concur with** Jim that the settlement is fair.

## connect to, connect with

> *connect to*—join (one object to another)
>
> The first step is to **connect** the positive wire **to** the positive pole.
>
> *connect with*—make contact with (a person, group, idea)
>
> If we drive overnight, we can **connect with** the first group by dawn.

## correspond to, correspond with

> *correspond to*—match
>
> The handwriting on this letter **corresponds to** the handwriting on the earlier document.
>
> *correspond with*—exchange messages
>
> Janet has **corresponded with** a friend in Costa Rica for three years.

## differ from, differ with

> *differ from*—be unlike
>
> The movie **differed from** the book in several ways.
>
> *differ with*—disagree with
>
> The figures in the government report **differ with** those in our study.

## inside, inside of

> *inside* (no preposition)—the part lying within
>
> I painted the **inside** wall of the kitchen.
>
> *inside of*—within (also used with expressions of time)
>
> The flower shop is **inside of** the building.
> He will return **inside of** an hour.

## in the market, on the market

*in the market*—looking to buy something

We're **in the market** for a great chocolate dessert.

*on the market*—up for sale

Hal put his house and boat **on the market** yesterday and hopes to sell them in a week.

## name

*name* (no preposition)—to appoint

Paula was **named** editor-in-chief of the *Los Angeles Chronicle*. (never "named as" editor-in-chief)

## outside, outside of

*outside* (no preposition)—the part lying without

I put the poster on the **outside** wall.

*outside of*—outside; except, other than

She went **outside of** the house. I can't think of anyone in the office, **outside of** Julio, who knows how to program this computer.

## promote, promote to

*promote* (with title, no preposition)—to increase in rank or status

She was **promoted** Lieutenant Commander.

*promote to*—to raise to a higher rank or status

She was **promoted to** executive level for her work in computer sales.

## reference to, reference on

*reference to*—a pointing toward

The governor made a **reference to** the pending legislation on low-income housing, calling it "long overdue."

*reference on*—books or articles about

Tarn's *Babylon* is a scholarly **reference on** the downfall of the Persian Empire.

## report of/on

*report of/on*—a written or verbal description (prepositions are used interchangeably)

He completed a 200-page **report on** why people prefer hand-held toothbrushes to electric ones.

## separate from

*separate from* (never separate out)—to divide; to distinguish

We'll have to **separate** the injured calf **from** the herd. Jerilyn's opinions are **separate from** her brother's.

## sympathy with, sympathy for

*sympathy with*—sharing another's feelings

I can **sympathize with** Jack; he has to babysit tonight.

*sympathy for*—having compassion for another

I feel **sympathy for** anyone who has lost a job.

## wait for, wait on, wait out

*wait for*—to be ready or at hand for

The general **waited for** the signal to attack.

*wait on*—to serve

When my father was in school, he earned money **waiting on** tables.

*wait out*—colloquial expression meaning to remain inactive during the course of

The fans **waited out** the rainstorm by taking shelter under the bleachers.

## write to

*write to*—send messages to (preposition is always used when direct object is missing)

I will **write to you** when you get to Chicago (direct object is missing). I will **write you** a note when you get to Chicago (direct object "note" is present).

# Appendix C. Frequently Confused Words

The meaning and spelling of the following words are commonly confused. Practice using them until the correct usage is familiar to you.

**accept, except**

> *accept*—to take, agree
>
> I **accept** the offer.
>
> *except*—excluding, omitting
>
> Everyone left **except** me.

**advice, advise**

> *advice*—opinion, counsel
>
> She needs your **advice.**
>
> *advise*—to counsel
>
> Please **advise** him of his rights.

**affect, effect**

> *affect*—to influence, change
>
> Inflation always **affects** our level of income.
>
> *effect*—(n.) impression, results; (v.) to cause
>
> The computer has had a profound **effect** on our everyday lives. It has **effected** a complete change in the way we do business.

**already, all ready**

> *already*—even now
>
> We **already** have a robot.
>
> *all ready*—all prepared
>
> They're **all ready** to go.

**assent, ascent**

> *assent*—(v.) to agree; (n.) permission
>
> Did they **assent** to your request? Yes, the entire board gave its **assent** to the project.
>
> *ascent*—advancement
>
> On the third day, they made their **ascent** to the top of Mount Everest.

## capital, capitol

*capital*—seat of government; wealth

The nation's **capital** braced itself for the holiday weekend. We need more **capital** to finance our new product line.

*capitol*—government building

They are putting a new roof on the **capitol.**

## cite, site, sight

*cite*—refer to, state

I **cited** my reasons for disagreeing.

*site*—location

The **site** for our home is lovely.

*sight*—scene

The city at dawn is a beautiful **sight.**

## cloths, clothes

*cloths*—pieces of cloth

Use soft **cloths** for polishing your silver.

*clothes*—wearing apparel

Every spring he buys new **clothes** and throws out the old ones.

## complement, compliment

*complement*—something that completes

Her humor is the perfect **complement** to my seriousness.

*compliment*—to say something good about someone; a flattering remark

My father always **compliments** my mother on her painting. The boss's **compliment** meant a lot to Carl.

## consul, council, counsel

*consul*—foreign embassy official

The Swedish **consul** threw a party for the president.

*council*—official body

The city **council** passed the ordinance by a three-to-one margin.

*counsel*—(v.) to advise; (n.) legal advisor

Find someone to **counsel** you about your accident. In fact, you should hire the company lawyer to act as **counsel** in this matter.

## dissent, descent, descend

*dissent*—disagreement

Mine was the only vote in **dissent** of the proposed amendment.

*descent*—a decline, fall

The road made a sharp **descent** then curved dangerously to the right.

*descend*—to come down

They had to **descend** from the mountain top in darkness.

## fewer, less

*fewer*—used for individual units, numbers

You will have to make **fewer** mistakes or order more erasers. We have five **fewer** donuts than we had this morning.

*less*—used for general quantities

The amount of money in our bank account is **less** than it was last year.

## formerly, formally

*formerly*—previously

I was **formerly** a typist.

*formally*—officially

She was sworn in **formally** as the fifth member of the panel.

## imply, infer

*imply*—to suggest

Are you **implying** that I was at the scene of the crime?

*infer*—to deduce from evidence

Your gloves were found in the room; thus, we **infer** that you visited the deceased sometime last night.

## it's, its

*it's*—contraction of it is or it has

**It's** (it has) been a long day. I've seen the play; **it's** (it is) not very good.

*its*—possessive form of the pronoun it

When the ship fired **its** guns, the blast was deafening.

## later, latter

*later*—after a time

They'll mail it **later** today.

*latter*—last mentioned of the two

If it's a choice between the beach and the mountains, I'll take the **latter**.

## lead, led, lead

*lead*—(v.) to go before; (adj.) first

The boys always **lead** the rush to the beach. The **lead** singer seems off tonight.

*led*—(v. past tense of lead) went before

They **led** the parade playing their kazoos.

*lead*—(n.) heavy metal; graphite

This paperweight is made of **lead.**

## lie, lay

*lie*—to rest or recline (lie, lay, lain)

The cat always **lies** down on my sweater. Yesterday he **lay** on it all day. I wish he had **lain** somewhere else.

*lay*—to put or place something (lay, laid, laid)

I **lay** the sweater on the couch. I **laid** it there without thinking about the cat. I have **laid** it there many times.

## lose, loose, loss

*lose*—misplace

Don't **lose** the tickets.

*loose*—not fastened down; release

The screw is **loose** on the showerhead. Turn the kids **loose** in the park.

*loss*—deprivation

His leaving was a **loss** to the company.

## past, passed

*past*—(n., adj.) preceding

The **past** president gave the gavel to the new president.

*passed*—(v.) went by; gone by

We **passed** my cousin on the road.

## personal, personnel

*personal*—individual

Can I ask you a **personal** question?

*personnel*—a department; workers

The human resources (**personnel**) office keeps records on all company **personnel**.

## precede, proceed

*precede*—to come before

My older brother **precedes** me by one grade in school.

*proceed*—to go ahead

We can **proceed** with our bake sale as soon as the weather clears.

## principle, principal

*principle*—rule, standard

Sound **principles** can help you make good decisions.

*principal*—main, chief; superintendent

She is the state's **principal** witness in this case. I'll never forget my grade school **principal,** Mr. Harvey.

## quiet, quite

*quiet*—silent

The valley is **quiet** at dusk.

*quite*—completely; to a considerable degree

He was **quite** upset with himself for losing the race. I **quite** agree that the judge was unfair.

## rise, raise

*rise*—(v.) to go up, to get up; (n.) reaction

The moon **rises** later each night. Your statement to the governor certainly got a **rise** out of him.

*raise*—(v.) to lift, bring up; (n.) an increase

**Raise** the picture a little higher. After four months, he finally got a **raise** in pay.

## sit, set

*sit*—to assume an upright position

We had to **sit** on the plane for three hours before we took off.

*set*—to put or place something

They **set** the coffee on the table. She **set** the files in order.

## stationary, stationery

*stationary*—still, fixed

The chair is **stationary.**

*stationery*—letter paper.

He took out a sheet of **stationery** and wrote a letter.

## than, then

*than*—after a comparison; when

Vivian is taller **than** Kelly. I no sooner started talking **than** Kelly interrupted me.

*then*—next; in that case

She took Fred's order, **then** mine. If you want to skip the mashed potatoes, **then** have the waitress mark it on the order.

## that, which

*that*—used to introduce a phrase or clause essential to the meaning of the sentence; the phrase or clause is not set off by commas

The shipment **that** arrived yesterday had to be returned. (*that arrived yesterday* identifies which shipment had to be returned and is essential information)

We ate the fifteen donuts **that** Jan brought to work this morning.

*which*—used to refer to a specific noun or pronoun and to introduce a phrase or clause **not** essential to the meaning of the sentence; the phrase or clause usually is set off by commas

We ate fifteen donuts, **which** was fifteen too many. (*which* refers to *donuts* and adds additional information *which was fifteen too many*)

The shipment, **which** arrived yesterday, had to be returned. (*which arrived yesterday* is incidental information and is set off by commas)

Exception: *That* or *which* can be used interchangeably to avoid too many repetitions of one word in a sentence.

## there, their, they're

*there*—a place

The book has to be on the table; I saw it **there** just a minute ago.

*their*—possessive form of they

Why don't they take **their** radios and go home?

*they're*—contraction of they are

**They're** upset that the watermelon fell off the table.

## weather, whether

*weather*—climate

The **weather** has been changing slowly over the past fifty years.

*whether*—if; regardless

They have to know **whether** you are going. You should tell them **whether** you feel like it or not.

## who's, whose

*who's*—contraction of who is or who has

Do you know **who's** (who is) coming to the party tonight? No, I don't know **who's** (who has) been invited.

*whose*—possessive form of who

**Whose** purple car is parked outside our house?

## you're, your

*you're*—contraction of you are

**You're** going to be late for dinner.

*your*—possessive form of you

**Your** dinner is cold.

# Appendix D. Frequently Misspelled Words

The following list contains words that are frequently misspelled. Use this list as a quick reference in addition to consulting a good dictionary.

## A

abbreviate
absence
abundant
accessible
accommodate
accompanies
accompaniment
accumulate
accuracy
acknowledgment
acquaintance
adequately
admission
admittance
adolescent
advantageous
allege
alliance
analysis
analyze
anonymous
apologetically
apparatus
apparent
appreciate
appropriate
argument
arrangement
arrears
ascertain
association
attendance
authorize
auxiliary
awfully

## B

ballet
bankruptcy
beneficial
bibliography
bookkeeper
boulevard
brochure
buffet
bulletin

## C

calculation
calendar
camouflage
canceled
cancellation
catalog/catalogue
catastrophe
category
cellar
cemetery
changeable
choose
chose
colossal
column
commitment
committed
committee
comparative
competent
competition
competitor
complexion

comptroller
conceivable
concise
conscience
conscientious
consciousness
consensus
consistency
contingency
controlling
controversy
correspondence
correspondents
criticize
curriculum

## D

debacle
debtor
decadent
deceitful
deference
deferred
dependent
depreciation
description
desirable
detrimental
dilemma
diligence
disastrous
disciple
discrimination
dissatisfied
division

## E

economical
ecstasy
effect
efficiency
embarrassment
emphasize
endeavor
enforceable
enormous
enthusiastically
entrance
espionage
exaggerate
excel
exceptionally
exhaustion
exhibition
exhibitor
exhilaration
existence
exorbitant
expensive
extension
exuberant

## F

facilitate
familiar
familiarize
fascination
feasible
feminine
financier
foreign
forfeit
franchise
fraud
fraudulent
freight
fulfill

## G

gauge
grammar
grievance
guarantee
guaranty
guidance

## H

harassment
hereditary
hindrance
horizontal
hygiene
hypocrisy
hypothetical

## I

ideally
idiomatic
illegible
immediately
imperative
implement
incidentally
inconvenience
indemnity
independent
indispensable
inevitable
inflationary
influential
ingenious
initial
initiative
innocent
inoculate
institution
intellectual
interference
interpretation
interrupt
invoice
irrelevant
irresistible
itemize
itinerary

## J

jeopardize
jeopardy
judgment/judgement

## K

kerosene
knowledge
knowledgeable

## L

labeled
laborious
larynx
legitimate
leisurely
liable
license
likelihood
livelihood
liquor
livable
loose
lose
lucrative
luxurious

## M

magistrate
magnificence
maintenance
majestic
malicious
manageable
mandatory
maneuver
marketable
marriageable
martyrdom
materialism
measurable
mediator
mediocre
melancholy
metaphor
miniature
miscellaneous
mischievous
misspell
misstatement
mortgage
mosquito
municipal
mysterious

## N

naive
necessity
negligible
negotiate
neurotic
neutral

ninety
ninth
noticeable

**O**

objectionable
observant
occasionally
occupant
occurrence
omission
omitting
opinionated
opportunity
option
outrageous
overrated

**P**

pageant
pamphlet
parallel
paralysis
parity
parliament
particularly
pastime
pedestal
penicillin
permanent
permissible
permitted
persistent
personal
personnel
perspiration
phenomenon
physician
picnicking
plausible
pneumonia
politician
possession
practically
precede
precise
preference
preferred
prejudice
presence
prestige
presumption

prevalent
privilege
procedure
propaganda
prophesy
prove
psychoanalysis
psychology
pursue

**Q**

qualitative
quality
quantitative
quantity
questionnaire
quietly
quit
quite

**R**

rebellion
receive
recommend
recommendation
reconciliation
recurrence
reducible
reference
referred
rehearsal
reimburse
relieve
reminiscent
remittance
remitted
repetition
representative
resource
respectfully
responsibility
returnable
reveal
revenue
routine

**S**

salable/saleable
schedule
scientific
scrutinize
separation

sergeant
serviceable
siege
significant
similar
souvenir
specifically
specimen
sponsor
statistics
strategic
stubbornness
substantial
succeed
succession
superficial
superfluous
superintendent
supersede
supervisor
suppress
surroundings
susceptible
symbolic
symmetrical
synonymous

**T**

tariff
technician
temperature
tendency
theoretical
tolerance
tomorrow
traffic
tragedy
transcend
transmit
transmittal
transparent
tried
twelfth
tyranny

**U**

unanimous
undoubtedly
uniform
universal
unmistakable
unnatural

unnecessary
unscrupulous

**V**

vaccine
vacuum
variation
vehicle
vengeance
ventilation
versatile
vigilance

villain
vinegar
volume

**W**

waive
warranty
welcome
whisper
whistle
wholly
withhold

**Y**

yacht
yawn
yield
young
youth

**Z**

zealous
zenith

# INDEX

# Correction Symbols

| | | | |
|---|---|---|---|
| **ad** | misuse of adverb or adjective | **'** | apostrophe |
| **adv** | adverb needed | **" "** | quotation marks |
| **agr** | faulty agreement | **. ? !** | period, question mark, exclamation point |
| **awk** | awkward | **- ( )** | dash, parentheses, |
| **cap** | capital letter | **[ ] ...** | brackets, ellipsis |
| **case** | error in case | **/** | slash |
| **coh** | coherence | **par, ¶** | new paragraph or |
| **coord** | faulty coordination | **no ¶** | no paragraph |
| **cs** | comma splice | **pass** | ineffective passive |
| **dev** | inadequate development | **plag** | plagiarism |
| **dm** | dangling modifier | **red** | redundant diction |
| **-ed** | error in **-ed** *ending* | **ref** | error in pronoun reference |
| **emph** | emphasis | **rev** | revise |
| **exact** | inexact language | **run-on** | run on sentence |
| **frag** | sentence fragment | **-s** | error in -s ending |
| **fs** | fused sentence | **shift** | distracting shift |
| **gg/us** | see glossary of usage | **sp** | misspelled word |
| **gr** | grammar | **sub** | faulty subordination |
| **hyph** | error in use of hyphen | **t/vt** | error in verb tense |
| **inc** | incomplete construction | **trans** | transition needed |
| **irreg** | error in irregular verb | **usage** | usage unacceptable |
| **ital** | italics (underlining) | **v** | voice |
| **logic** | logic faulty | **var** | lack of variety in sentence structure |
| **lc** | use lowercase letter | | |
| **mixed** | mixed construction | **vb** | error in verb form |
| **mm** | misplaced modifier | **w** | wordy |
| **mood** | error in mood | **wo** | write out abbreviation or number |
| **ms** | manuscript form | | |
| **nonst** | nonstandard usage | **ww** | wrong word/faulty word choices |
| **num** | error in use of number | **/ /** | faulty parallelism |
| **om** | omitted word | **/** | (on letter) use lower case |
| **order** | sentences not in most effective order | | (between letters) separate |
| | | **^** | insert |
| **p/pr** | error in punctuation | **x** | obvious error |
| **⸲** | comma | **#** | insert space |
| **no,** | no comma | **◡** | close up |
| **;** | semicolon | **≡** | (under letter) capitalize |
| **:** | colon | | |